# Mitsubishi
# A5M (Claude)
## carrier borne fighter

STRATUS

Published in Poland in 2003 by STRATUS
Artur Juszczak, Po. Box 123, 27-600 Sandomierz 1, Poland
*e-mail: arturj@mmpbooks.biz*
for
Mushroom Model Publications,
36 Ver Road, Redbourn,
AL3 7PE, UK.
*e-mail: rogerw@waitrose.com*

© 2003 Mushroom Model Publications.
http://www.mmpbooks.biz



## ISBN 83-917178-0-1

| | |
|---|---|
| *Editor in chief* | Roger Wallsgrove |
| *Editors* | Bartłomiej Belcarz<br>Robert Pęczkowski<br>Artur Juszczak |
| *Edited by* | Robert Pęczkowski |
| *Page design by* | Artur Juszczak<br>Robert Pęczkowski |
| *Cover Layout* | Artur Juszczak |
| *DTP* | Robert Pęczkowski<br>Artur Juszczak |
| *Translation* | Wojtek Matusiak |
| *Proofreading* | Roger Wallsgrove |
| *Colour Drawings* | Zygmunt Szeremeta |
| *Scale plans* | Andrzej Gorcziński |
| *All photos* | Author's collection |

*Printed by: Drukarnia Diecezjalna,
ul. Żeromskiego 4,
27-600 Sandomierz
tel. (15) 832 31 92;
fax (15) 832 77 87
www.wds.pl
marketing@wds.pl*

**PRINTED IN POLAND**

# Table of contents

# Introduction

On the morning of 20 September 1937 the largest circulation Japanese daily newspaper, Asahi Shimbun, followed by other papers, announced sensational news from the Chinese-Japanese front. They reported that the previous day, flying their first combat missions, a dozen brand new monoplane fighters of the Imperial Japanese Naval Aviation branch had claimed an outstanding success. Within 15 minutes over Nanking, the Chinese capital, they destroyed no less than 33 enemy fighters for no losses. It would later turn out that the enemy losses quoted were a little inflated, and the air combat lasted longer than 15 minutes, but even the true outcome of the encounter was still impressive.

During the first eleven weeks of the so called "Chinese Incident", starting in July 1937, the Imperial Japanese Army made significant progress. Peiping and Tientsin fell quickly, but logistics problems due to the long distances involved resulted in a slowing down of the offensive, while Chinese resistance in Shanghai became stronger. During that time the Imperial Japanese Navy also managed to secure local air superiority in some areas, even though it used obsolete Nakajima A2N fighters, operating from the light aircraft carrier Hosho patrolling the sea off Shanghai. These forces were reinforced on 15 August, when the much larger carrier Kaga arrived off the Chinese coast. At that time the carrier was equipped with the older A2N, too, but within a week its force was complemented by two modern Mitsubishi A5M2 monoplane fighters which flew their first mission on 22 August. The pilots were unable to demonstrate their superiority during the first operational flight as they encountered no opposition. It took until

*First prototype of the Claude. Mitsubishi Ka-14.*

4th September to display the abilities of the new aeroplanes. That day two A5M2 fighters, led by Lt. Tadashi Nakajima, encountered several Chinese Hawk II and Hawk III aircraft over Lake Dahu. Lt. Nakajima and his wingman downed three of the Chinese fighters, and returned safely to Kaga.

Meanwhile, on 11 July the 13 Kokutai (Air Corps) was formed, which included 12 Mitsubishi A5M fighters and 18 Aichi D1A and Yokosuka B4Y bombers. On 9 September these forces landed at Gong Da airfield near Shanghai. Their task was to soften the defences along the Japanese attack lines southwards, along the railway line to Nanking, which was attacked on 19 September by Naval aircraft. This was the 10th day of the Japanese aerial offensive against various targets in the outskirts of the Chinese capital. The airfields, which housed most of the Chinese Air Force, were the main target. For these actions the 12 A5M aircraft of the 13 Kokutai based at Gong Da airfield were reinforced with six A5Ms from the carrier Kaga. Thus all eighteen A5M fighters were ready to be used from the first day of the offensive, as an escort for the Naval bombers. On the first day of the offensive these aircraft, led by Lt. Shichiro Yamashita, flew two missions over the Chinese capital, encountering some 50 Chinese Hawk III and Boeing 281 aircraft. Upon return the Japanese pilots claimed 26 enemy fighters for no losses. This was the combat leading to the exaggerated newspaper reports.

Japanese abilities in aircraft design and construction were largely neglected in Western countries. The Japanese aircraft industry was commonly labelled as only able to copy, and both its technology and the quality of the military equipment was considered to be far behind similar Western designs. It took the first air combats of the A5M aircraft over the Chinese capital to prove that a Japanese developed aeroplane was in every respect superior to the aircraft of the opposing

*Photo of the Claude prototype under close examination.*

force, the latter mainly relying on combat aircraft of Western design (albeit not "state-of-the-art"). Nevertheless, the advance of Japanese military technology remained unnoticed in the West. Looking back at the events of those days, one can consider them a prelude to those that would follow in the Pacific four years later, when an aeroplane from the same design office, based on the same concept, became a legend: the Zero fighter, considered initially by its enemies to posses some mystical qualities. Although the new Mitsubishi A5M fighter, introduced in late summer 1937 into the air war over China, did not have its excellent performance from the outset, it showed Japan could achieve world-class design and production levels.

Product of the ambitious 9-Shi specification (1934) which called for high performance without stipulating how it was to be achieved, the A5M was world's first production single-seat carrier-borne fighter built as a cantilever monoplane. In other respects, as well, it was original, and was one of the most agile monoplanes ever built. The A5M possessed biplane advantages implemented in a monoplane: particularly high dog-fighting ability, this being the most prized air combat tactic in Japan.

In February 1934, Kaigun Koku Hombu (Naval Aviation Headquarters) issued, among other requirements for the 9-Shi development programme, a specification for a single-seat fighter. The document did not specify that this should be a carrier-borne fighter, just a fighter as such. It had been assumed that the naval aviation could not use an aeroplane that was not designed from the start for carrier operations, and therefore earlier requirements included performance-sapping requirements. Lieutenant Commander Hideo Sawai, who played a major role in the preparation of these new specifications, believed that he could stimulate designers to create an aeroplane with performance largely exceeding that of carrier-borne aeroplanes designed in the old way. According to Sawai, first an excellent land-based fighter would be

*Another view of the Mitsubishi Ka-14. Note the gull wing.*

developed, and only then would it be modified for carrier operations. He was persuaded that in order to achieve perfect results of the design process, the requirements should specify only the features linked with excellent fighter characteristics. Sawai believed that the problem of adopting the fighter for carrier operations was better subject to separate specifications, after a proper fighter had been built. This radical move resulted in the 9 Shi specification. This document quoted only the performance requirements. Those principal ones were: maximum speed of 350 km/h at an altitude of 3,000 m; ability to climb to 5,000 m within 6.5 minutes; total fuel tank capacity no less than 240 litres; armament consisting of two 7.7 mm machine guns; a radio set; overall dimensions not exceeding 11 m in span and 8 m in length.

The task to turn the 9-Shi specifications into reality was entrusted to Jiro Horikoshi at the Mitsubishi design office, as the leading designer under the general supervision of Jyoji Hattori. Mr Horikoshi and his team faced a tough task in fulfilling the specification while developing a new aeroplane of exemplary aerodynamic cleanness. Only the most conservative minds would opt for a layout other than cantilever monoplane, and this decided the concept for the most advanced project. In order to meet the 9-Shi specification for a fighter aeroplane, the team chose light alloy monocoque structure with stressed skin. A fuselage, of minimum cross-section area, was connected to a two-spar wing (tubular profile spar). This elliptical wing was an inverted gull-wing section or W-shaped in head-on view, with anhedral ($16.4^\circ$) from the fuselage to the undercarriage attachment, and dihedral ($9.5^\circ$) outboard. A thin wing airfoil was selected, 16 percent thickness at the root and 9 percent at the tip. Special attention was paid to aerodynamic cleanliness, hence the use of countersunk rivets and inspection panel fasteners.

The Nakajima Kotobuki 5 (Congratulation) 9-cylinder air cooled radial with reduction gear, rated at 550 hp for take off and 600 hp at

*Second protoype of Ka-14 without the gull wing.*

3,100 m, was selected as the optimum power plant. It was also lighter than the Mitsubishi Kinsei A-4 which offered similar performance. Retractable undercarriage was considered, but calculations showed that the 10 percent gain obtained this way in terms of drag would only result in a maximum speed increase of some 3 percent, this achieved at the cost of increased weight and complicated undercarriage design. It was also feared that this could delay the entire programme. The W-form wing had been suggested by Commander Jiro Saba in the earlier 7-Shi specification for a fighter aeroplane, as a means of improving cockpit visibility during deck landing, but already at an early stage of the 9-Shi project some calculations indicated faults in this solution. There were reasons to believe that turbulent airflow would be generated by the anhedral/dihedral transition, which could affect the characteristics of the aeroplane. It was therefore decided that, in order to carry out comparative trials, one of two prototype aircraft, designated Ka-14 by the manufacturer, would be fitted with the W-wing, and the other with a standard wing.

Assembly of the first prototype Ka-14 aeroplane was completed in January 1935, within eleven months from the issue of the 9-Shi specification. The problem of the aeroplane weight, specially focused during design of the complete structure, proved less than expected. On the other hand, lack of experience in countersunk riveting resulted in some skin unevenness, and small perforations were noticed around the rivets, so the surface of the entire aeroplane was filled and polished. Soon afterwards the Ka-14 aeroplane was shipped to Kagamigahara base, some 15 miles north of Nagoya, where the first flight trials took place. On 4 February 1935 Mitsubishi test pilot Kajima made the first flight. The take-off weight of the Ka-14 was 1,373 kg, resulting in a wing loading of 77.2 kg/m$^2$, rather high by Japanese standards of the time. Four months later, on 22 May 1935, several thousand miles to the west, at Augsburg-Haunstetten airfield in Bavaria, the prototype of another fighter aeroplane was subjected to similar flying trials. This was the Messerschmitt Bf 109V1 fighter, progenitor of a new generation of fighter aeroplanes, dramatically differing in its principal assumptions from the rules observed in Japan. The German prototype, although its engine power output was just 7 percent higher than that of the Kotobuki 5 engine in the Ka-14, had wing loading over 50 percent higher than that of the Japanese fighter, reaching 117.18 kg/m$^2$.

First trial results of the prototype Ka-14 fulfilled the expectations of its designer, Horikoshi, and his team, and it became clear that the 9-Shi specification was not only met but exceeded. The pilot Kajima reported after the first flight that the stability and manoeuvrability of the aeroplane were excellent, and the main shortcomings were longitudinal oscillations of the aeroplane at high angles of attack, and the tendency to drop a wing during landing. During further trials a maximum speed of 444 km/h at an altitude of 3,200 m was achieved, this being performance that previously Japanese naval aviation could only dream of.

Lt. Com. Yoshio Kobayashi from the Naval Aviation Board (later Naval Aviation Research and Development Centre) was posted to lead the trials of the new aeroplane on behalf of the Kaigun Koku Hombu. He moved to live at the Nagarahawa Hotel in the town of Gifu, not far from the airfield at Kagamigahara, where he developed the flying trial programme for the Yokosuka Kotutai, experimental air unit that tested new naval aircraft. Initially it was planned that the trials would be carried out at Oppama basc, but when it was realised that the gliding angle and pitching of the Ka-14 could be dangerous for the prototype, it was decided that the airfield at Oppama was too small and the original concept was revived, to have the flying trials at Kamigahara airfield under supervision from the naval aviation representatives, chiefly Lt. Com. Yoshio Kobayashi. It was he that made several challenging flights in the Ka-14 prototype at an altitude of 2,150 m, with recorded speed of 397 km/h, and achieved a speed of 449 km/h at an altitude of 3,200 m. During measurements of the rate-of-climb he reached 5,000 m in 5.9 minutes. Yoshio Kobayashi confirmed the excellent flight stability of the prototype, and its manoeuvrability. In order to assess its combat capability the Ka-14 prototype was allocated to the "Genda Circus" at Yokosuka Kokutai in Yokosuka. The unit, commanded by Lieutenant Minoru Genda, included the then best naval pilots, their task being to perform comparative tests of the Ka-14 prototype in mock combat against other fighters. The comparison flights, which also included the second Ka-14 prototype, were carried out during the autumn of 1935 on unfavourable terms, for the old habits of the naval pilots who paid more attention to manoeuvrability than anything else. The Ka-14 was extremely manoeuvrable for a monoplane, but in a conventional dog-fight it was significantly inferior to the much lighter and more manoeuvrable Nakajima A4N1 biplane that equipped the naval aviation before the 9-Shi specification was drawn. After flying both aircraft in a simulated air combat against each other, Minoru Genda named the A4N1 as the better aeroplane to achieve local air superiority. His deputy, commander of the "Genda Circus" Lieutenant Ryosuke Nomura, supported Genda's opinion, as did other Navy pilots who participated in the comparative trials. Their belief in the overall superiority of the A4N1 was unfounded, but remained until a change in air combat tactics to climb and attack was made. This change in tactics reversed the conclusions from previous trials, and convinced the Navy pilots of the Ka-14's abilities. Even Minoru Genda, eager supporter of biplanes, later became enthusiastic about the Mitsubishi monoplane.

The second prototype Ka-14, which joined flying trials during late spring of 1937, differed from its predecessor in many respects. The most important one was the change from a W-shaped wing. At a late stage of construction of the second prototype it was decided to add flaps in the centre wing section, copied from those in a Northrop 2E imported to Japan. Fitting these was intended to improve the landing characteristics of the Ka-14. The wing design also incorporated a change that expanded laminar flow over the wing tip, improving stability at high angles of attack. These changes led to a drop in speed of a mere 2.75 km/h. Low stability at high angles manifested itself by wing slip, and it was cured by extending the pilot's headrest along the entire fuselage, to form an additional dorsal fin. Problems with the unimpressive reduction gear of the Kotobuki 5 engine were solved by replacing it with the direct-drive Kotobuki 3, turning the two-bladed propeller at engine speed. The engine produced a take-off output of 640 hp, and 715 hp at 2,800 m. Flying trials of the second prototype Ka-14 showed that, despite the weight growing to 1,470 kg, the performance was virtually unchanged, only the time to reach 5,000 m rose by 5 seconds. All the control faults were eliminated, and both controllability and manoeuvrability were improved. In order to test other radial engines, such as the Nakajima Hikari 1, and Mitsubishi Konsei A8 and A-9, and also in order to optimise the control surfaces, Kaigun Koku Hombu ordered four more prototypes, respectively customised to define the optimum elevator area, this being achieved at 26.5 percent of the tailplane area. Meanwhile a trials programme to reduce frontal engine drag was commenced using the Ka-14. The wide Townend ring was replaced with a flush fitting cowling that reached over the forward fuselage. Individual cylinder pushrods were housed in separate fairings, and each cylinder was fitted with an individual exhaust pipe. This failed to produce the anticipated results and the wide annular cowling was accepted as standard. After these trials the first prototype Ka-14 was allocated for destructive static tests.

As soon as the Kaigun Koku Hombu expressed satisfaction with the performance of the 9 Shi fighter, the Koku Hombu (Army Air Force Headquarters) ordered an example, designated Ki-18. Essentially the aeroplane was similar to the second prototype Ka-14, but with the Kotobuki 5 engine with reduction gear, wide engine cowling, slightly enlarged rudder, and larger undercarriage wheels, legs and spats. The Ki-18 underwent extensive trials during late autumn and winter of 1935 in the Army Air Force Technical Institute at Tachikawa and at the Flying Testing Centre at Akeno. Although the Ki-18 failed to find approval of the Army Air Force pilots, still it provoked the Koku Hombu in June 1935 to prepare a specification for an advanced fighter, able to achieve better performance than the Ki-18 and possessing excellent manoeuvrability. The companies invited to compete included Kawasaki, Mitsubishi, and Nakajima, and after a while all presented prototypes of their aircraft for comparative trials. The Koku Hombu expected that Mitsubishi would offer an extensively redesigned fighter, but with its personnel busy working on the development of the Ka-14 in preparation for series production, only a small amount of time was devoted to reshaping of the Ki-18, which was re-submitted for testing as the Ki-33, to compete against the Ki-28 and Ki-27, from Kawasaki and Nakajima respectively. The Ki-33 was powered by a Nakajima Ha-1a engine developed from the Kotobuki 3 and had a rating of 710 hp for take-off and 775 hp at 3,700 m. The aeroplane featured a cockpit hood partly slid back, raised rear fuselage, the wide engine cowling, and more changes to the fin. In other respects it was similar to the Ki-18. Comparative trials between the prototypes commenced at Tachikawa in November 1936 and continued into the early spring of 1937. The Ki-33 was beaten, although not by much, by the Nakajima Ki-27 which entered service with the Army Air Force as the "Type 97 Army fighter".

*First prototype of A5M4 (Ka-14) with inverted gull-wing section, upper view.*

# A5M1

**M**itsubishi were not too disappointed with their failure in the advanced Army fighter competition, as its production line at Nagoya was filled with fighters for the Navy. By late autumn 1936 the Ka-14 had successfully undergone all the pre-planned trials, and the new aeroplane was officially approved for series production for the Imperial Japanese Naval Aviation as the "Type 96 carrier-borne naval fighter Model 1" (A5M1). Production A5M1 Model 1 aircraft were essentially similar to the second prototype Ka-14, except for the re-designed engine cowling, increased capacity of the internal tanks for greater range, and the rear fuselage. The A5M1 was powered by the Kotobuki 2 Kai A, rated at 580 hp for take-off and 630 hp at 1,500 m. Internal fuel capacity rose to 330 litres, compared to 200 litres in the prototype, by adding two 68 litre tanks in the outer wing panels.

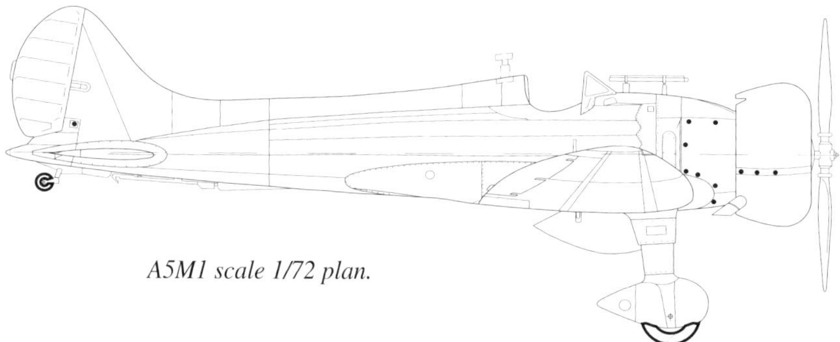

*A5M1 "3-151" personal aircraft of PO3c Katsuhiro Hashimoto, 12th Kokutai. Note the rear part of the wheel cover has been removed.*

*A5M1 scale 1/72 plan.*

*In the foreground Navy Type 96 Carrier Fighter, Model 1 (A5M1) "31" of the 12th Kokutai at Gungdai Air Base near Shanghai, China in March 1938. Personal aircraft of PO3c Hitoshi Sato. In the background Model 2-1 "32" flown by PO3c Shigeru Makino.*

**Left:**
*A5M1 in flight.*

**Below:**
*A5M1 "3-133" of 12 Kokutai, China, 1938.*

The armament consisted of two 0.303 in. Type 89 machine guns fitted in the upper fuselage over the engine with 500 rounds per gun. Overall weight of the aeroplane rose to 1,500 kg, resulting in increased wing loading of 84.2 kg/$m^2$. This led to reduced performance, mainly due to the use of a less powerful engine, additional equipment, and more fuel. Maximum speed reached 406 km/h at an altitude of 2,100 m, climb to 5,000 metres took 8.5 minutes. Before the design team started working on reviving the performance of the proto-type, units took delivery of 75 produc-tion A5M1 Model 1 aircraft. One of the first production aircraft was built as the A5M1a, experimentally fitted with two 20 mm Oerlikon FF cannon.

***Above:***
*Nakajima Kotobuki 2 Kai 1 9-cylinder air-cooled radial engin*

*Right:*
*A5M1, with anti nose-over pylon.*

***Below, right:***
*Drawing of A5M1 canopy.*

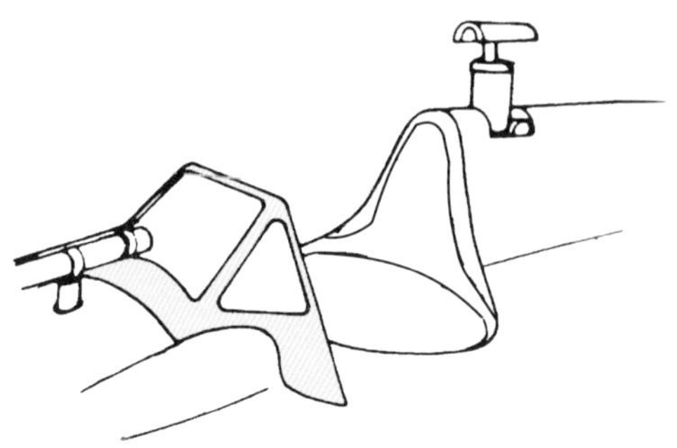

# A5M2

I n order to achieve the required characteristics, the designers used the improved Kotobuki 2 Kai 3A engine with a longer cowling, which had a rating of 610 hp for take-off and 690 hp at 3900 m and drove a 2.98 m diameter three-bladed propeller in place of the previous 2.69 m dia. two-bladed propeller. Exhaust pipes were shortened, and the carburettor air intake was split into two inlets located

*A5M2a (early) 1/72 scale plan, side view.*

*A5M2a (late) 1/72 scale plan, side view.*

*A5M2a, 1/72 scale plan, front view.*

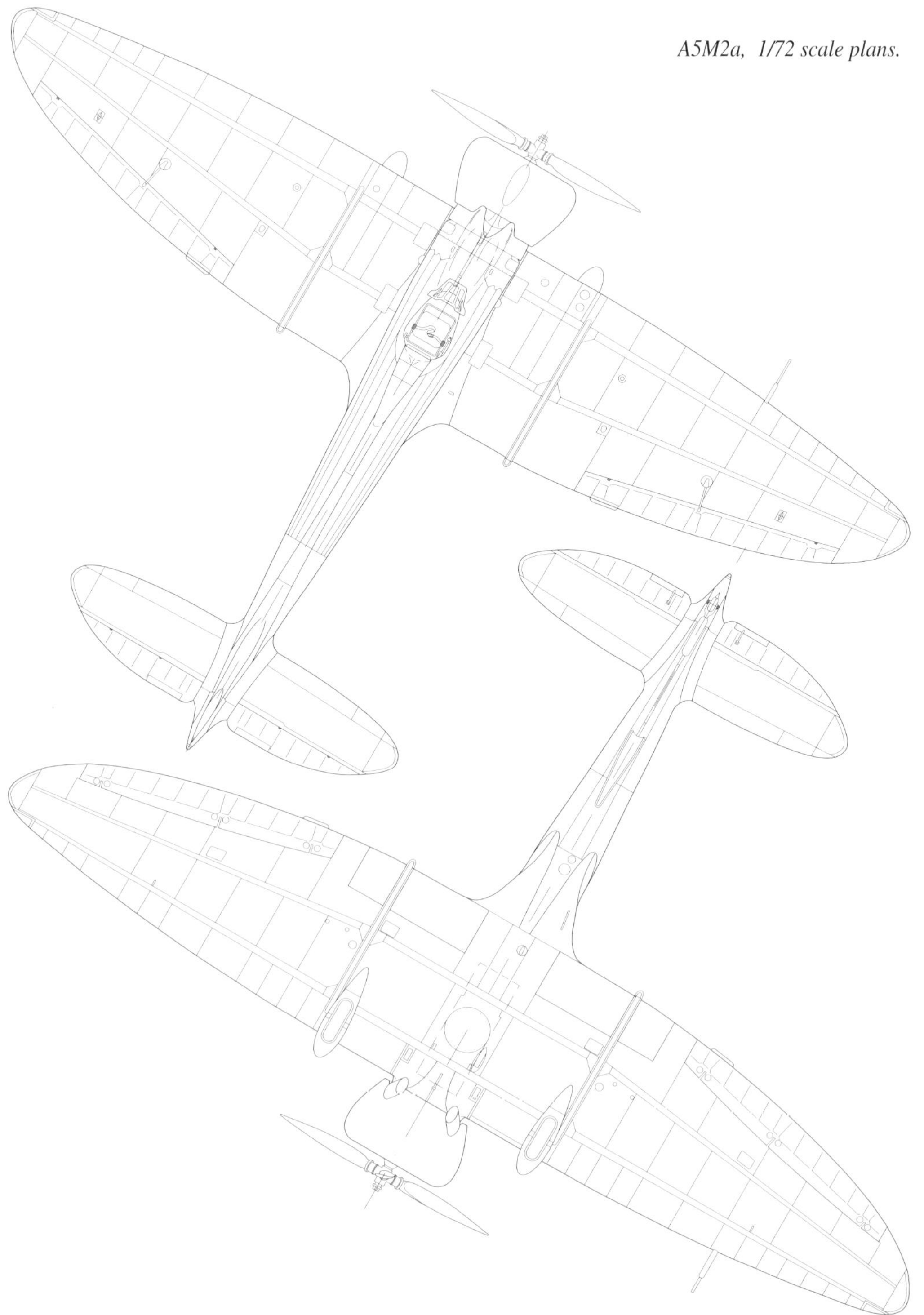


A5M2a,  1/72 scale plans.

on the port and starboard sides of the cockpit, slightly obscuring forward visibility. The dorsal fin was altered and slightly deepened, and in order to maintain the centre of gravity the engine mount was shortened by 165 mm. After these changes the production aircraft were designated A5M2a Model 2-1. This version started to leave the production lines at the end of spring 1937. Maximum speed rose to 426 km/h at 3,090 m and the climb to 5,000 m was made in 7.98 minutes, but the overall weight was increased to 1,608 kg, and wing loading to 89.9 kg/m$^2$. The increase of these latter figures affected the manoeuvrability of the aeroplane.

The beginning of the "Chinese Incident" on 7 July 1937 led to an accelerated delivery of A5M fighters to operational units. As mentioned before, the first fighters of the type were taken on charge by the 13th Kokutai a mere four days later. After the entirely successful first air combats over Nanking, starting from 19 September, the A5M aircraft of the 13th Kokutai and those transferred from the aircraft carrier Kaga entered full-scale combat, playing the main role in the air offensive against the Chinese capital city, although by that time the resistance of the Chinese fighters was significantly weaker. On 20, 22, and 26 September, the Japanese monoplanes scored four victories for no losses. After this the aircraft carrier returned to

*A5M2 with wheel cover partially removed. Note 160 l additional fuel tank.*

*A5M2 of 12 Kokutai, China, 1938.*

A5M2. This aircraft was later rebuilt into the A5M3 with inline engine.

the South China Sea, where it remained until the end of 1938, except for a short spell in November 1937 when it was sent to Shanghai in order to provide air cover during landing operations.

At the same time, as of 3 October, 13th Kokutai carried out the second air offensive against Nanking, during which the A5M fighters participated in 27 missions within three weeks, encountering varying resistance from the Chinese defenders. For example, on 6 October ten A5M aircraft fought two air battles against 23 Chinese fighters, scoring 9 victories for no losses. Six days later eleven Japanese A5M fighters fought against seven Chinese fighters, enjoying supremacy in numbers for the first time. This time 5 Chinese aircraft were shot down, but the Japanese lost three fighters. It was later explained that the loss of these aircraft was due to the fact that their pilots were inexperienced and mistook the Chinese Breda 27 aircraft for friendly aircraft. On 14 October A5M aircraft avenged the loss in combat against eleven Chinese aircraft, shooting down two with no losses.

By that time the 12th Kokutai, which had been formed in parallel with the 13th Kokutai, but with 12 Nakajima A4N1 biplanes, started to receive A5M aircraft as reinforcements. This corps took part in the second battle of Shanghai, during which the Chinese posed fierce resistance against the Japanese landing. A4N1s were introduced in combat as attack aircraft and as base escorts, but from 8 November on, after the capture of Shanghai, they started to be replaced with the A5Ms. A5M aircraft of both Kokutais took part in supporting the troops landing in the Hanzhou bay, flying patrol missions, escorting

A5M2, of 12 Kokutai, 1938. Note the *anti nose-over pylon in extended position.*

the transport ships, and attacking ground targets. In this case the Chinese resistance in the air was very weak, and the only air combat with participation of A5M aircraft took place on 11 November, when three A5Ms from the aircraft carrier Kaga intercepted three Chinese Northrop 2Es that attempted to attack Kaga. Two of the Chinese bombers were shot down.

Following the capture of Shanghai, the Japanese forces moved up the Yangtze river, towards Nanking. Resistance of the Chinese on land was not very strong, but the air resistance over the capital city and over the city of Nanchang that now became the main target of the Japanese troops became much stronger, mainly by the introduction of four Soviet "volunteer" fighter units under Stepan P. Suprun. These units were equipped with Polikarpov I-152 biplane and Polikarpov I-16 monoplanes, arriving at Nanking at the last moment to reinforce the largely weakened defence before the third and last Japanese air offensive against Nanking that commenced on 20 November. During the offensive which continued until the fall of Nanking, from 13 until 22 December the A5M fighters of the 12th and 13th Kokutai and from the aircraft carrier Kaga were employed to escort Hiro G2H1 and Mitsubishi G3M2 bomb-

*A5M2 "4-122" of 13th Kokutai, supposedly flown by Lt. Shigeru Takuma when he was killed in action on 25 February, 1938.*

*Left:*
*Drawing of A5M2b canopy.*

***Below:***
A5M2b "3-154"of 12 Kokutai, with 210 l additional tank,

*A5M2b of an unknown unit.*

ers. During this stage of fighting the A5M aircraft scored 38 air kills. Soviet I-152 fighters assigned to defend Nanking and Nanchang, as well as I-16 fighters, scored a few kills and achieved local air superiority. It is hard to choose the  between the A5M and I-152, if they were flown by similarly experienced pilots. In a classic dog-fight an average Japanese pilot was better trained than his Soviet counterpart, and the latter used the advantage of greater weight and armour of their aircraft. Soviet fighters were a tough opponent for the A5M aircraft, armed with just two light machine guns, so during the last 10 days of November the number of air victories achieved

*Right:*
*Nakajima Kotobuki 2 Kai 3b 9-cylinder air-cooled radial engine.*

*Below:*
*A5M2b of Hyakurihara Kokutai .*

by Navy pilots fell dramatically. Only two kills were scored on 22 November, and two more two days later, in spite of a large number of encounters.

*Another view of A5M2b of Hyakurihara Kokutai.*

A5M pilots soon learned the combat value of the Soviet-flown aircraft, but on 2 December they scored seven kills, including three of the newly-introduced Tupolev SB bombers that attacked Japanese positions on the outskirts of Nanking. This encounter was the first that involved twenty Soviet I-16 fighters against A5M aircraft of the 13th Kokutai under Lieutenant Mochifumi Nangoh. The Japanese suffered no losses. Their success was made possible by the lack of experience of the Russians, and also because the A5M aircraft proved more manoeuvrable than the I-16s, both in horizontal and vertical combat. Either way, the strength of the A5M structure was a nice sur-

*A5M2 "4-122" of 13th Kokutai, supposedly flown by Lt. Shigeru Takuma, see also page 19.*

*A5M2b, China, 1938, with bomb racks.*

*A5M2, 12 Kokutai, October 1937.*

prise even for the Japanese. Mitsubishi A5M fighters were able to stand even very extensive damage from the Soviet large-calibre machine guns. This structural strength was dramatically demonstrated on 9 December during combat over Nanchang, when the A5M of Warrant Officer Kanichi Kashimura from the 13th Kokutai collided with a Chinese Hawk III. The Japanese aeroplane lost a third of the wing, but Kashimura managed to reach his base. This achievement was a proud one for the manufacturer, as in addition, throughout the service of these aircraft there was not a single case of an accident due to a design fault. The air combat during which Kashimura lost a portion of his wing was fought by seven A5M aircraft of the 13th Kokutai, again led by Lieutenant Nongoh, against twenty Chinese and Soviet fighters. Twelve enemy aircraft were shot down for the loss of one A5M. Two weeks later, on 22 December, twelve A5Ms of the 13th Kokutai and from the aircraft carrier Kaga, led by Lieutenant Norito Obbayashi, again scored a dozen kills over Nanchang, but during the combat Obbayashi was killed following a collision with an I-16.

After the capture of Nanking the Japanese government expected the Chinese authorities to fall and resistance at the front line to grow weaker, but Chang Kai-Shek moved his capital further west, to Hankow. In spite of large losses suffered by the Chinese, they still showed the will to fight both on land and in the air, the latter mainly thanks to reinforcement of their air force with 93 I-152 aircraft in early 1938 and 93 more aircraft during subsequent months. After the capture of Shantung, the Japanese continued their air attacks against Nanchang, but this time they paid more attention to Hankow. Therefore,

from the beginning of January 1938, Japanese naval aviation increased the rate of attacks on these cities. A5M aircraft were used mainly to escort bombers. On 4 January, during the battle over Hankow, sixteen A5Ms of the 12th and 13th Kokutais fought against twenty I-152 and I-16 aircraft, shooting down four for no losses. Three days later Lieutenant Ryohei Ushioda, leader of the fighter group of the 12th Kokutai, lost his life in an attack against the airfield at Nanchang.

During the first four months of the "Chinese Incident" losses among Navy fighters were very low, considering the rate of combat operations. At the same time the first aces achieved scores of 10 or more air victories. They would later return to Japan for propaganda reasons. One of them was Warrant Officer Kiyozumi Koga of the 13th Kokutai, who participated in six major air battles, scoring his first kill over Nanking on 19 September 1937. He returned to Japan in December 1937 with a score of 13 victories, and became a test pilot at Yokosuka Kokutai. He was killed in an accident on 15 September 1938.

Mitsubishi A5M fighters and their pilots confirmed their air superiority during

*Above:*
*A5M2a of 13 Kokutai.*
*Below:*
*A5M2b of 12 Kokutai, with a foundation inscription, 25 October 1938.*
*Bottom:*
*A5M2b of 12 Kokutai, 1938. Aircraft with 210 l tank.*

the battle over Hankow on 18 February 1938, when eleven A5Ms of the 12th and 13th Kokutais, while escorting G3M2 bombers, were intercepted by eighteen I-152 and eighteen I-16 aircraft. Two of the I-16s and four I-152s were shot down for the loss of four A5M aircraft, including that flown by Lieutenant Tadashi Kaneko, who had succeeded Lieutenant Ryohei Ushioda as commander of the 12th Kokutai fighter group. A week later the next commander, Lieutenant Shigeo Takuma, was shot down together with another A5M pilot when eighteen A5M fighters of the 12th and 13th Kokutais encountered no less than 50 I-152 and I-16 aircraft over Nanchang, scoring 27 kills. It was during that combat that Warrant Officer Tetsuo Iwamoto, who became the top ace of the Imperial Japanese Naval Aviation, scored 5 victories during his first air combat.

On 25 January 1938 a formation of 12 Chinese SB bombers carried out a high altitude attack against the airfield at Nanking, the principal base of the Japanese naval aviation in that area. Although Nakajima A4N1 aircraft patrolled the airfield area at the time, the SBs achieved a total success, leaving on the ground two burnt-out and several damaged G3M2 bombers. The A4N1 biplane fighters did not have enough performance to intervene effectively. However, when eight A5Ms were scrambled, they managed to catch the bombers on the way back and shoot down one of these. This raid stressed the urgency of deliveries of the new fighter to China.

The Mitsubishi aircraft factory at Nagoya faced problems with maintaining the rate of deliveries of new aircraft, and this resulted from the increased pace of combat operations in China. The aircraft carrier Soryu, completed in August 1937, took position off the central Chinese coast. It had eighteen obsolete A4N1 fighters, due to slow deliveries of the A5M. The replacement A5Ms soon arrived, though, and in early April 1938 nine A4N1 aircraft were sent to Nanking in order to reinforce the air defence of the capital city. The same month the 13th Kokutai withdrew to Shanghai due to combat losses, having passed its remaining A5M aircraft to the 12th Kokutai. In April the 14th Kokutai was formed in Japan with 12 A5M fighters and 24 bombers. The unit was deployed to the island of Sanzao, near Macao, in order to support operations in South China. Two months later, in June 1938, the 15th Kokutai was forming, but lack of A5M aircraft resulted in the unit being equipped with both the new A5M fighters and the obsolete A4N1s. Initially the unit was deployed to Anking, where A5M aircraft sent to that area from the aircraft carrier Soryu had operated since April. Later, in September, 15th Kokutai was moved to Yiyang, attacking Hankow from there. During that time the remaining A4N1 fighters were withdrawn and replaced by A5Ms. At that time the fighter group from the aircraft carrier

*Pilot seat used on early Claude versions.*

Kaga, without significant experience in air combat, operated in the South China Sea area. On 13 April six A5M carrier-borne fighters, while escorting Aichi D1A and Yokosuka B4Y bombers during an attack against Canton, were intercepted by a mixed Chinese formation of 20 Gloster Gladiator* and Hawk III aircraft that had taken off from Tien Ho airfield. This time the A5Ms scored 11 victories for no losses. A few months later, on 30 August, A5Ms from the aircraft carrier Kaga, in an air battle with Gladiators over Nantsiong, shot down sixteen for the loss of two aircraft.

While the carrier-borne A5M fighters of the Japanese naval aviation fought bloody combats over China, Mitsubishi worked hard on further development of the type, commencing assembly of a new variant, the A5M2b Model 2-2. This new version reverted to the Kotobuki 3 engine that had been fitted in the second Ka-14 prototype. This time it was cowled with a wide NACA ring, fitted with gills and featuring a flattened top to improve visibility. The carburettor air intake was repositioned, and a number of minor changes resulting from combat experiences in China were introduced. These included attachments and the necessary systems for two 30 kg bombs, but the most important change was the larger diameter fuselage and a completely enclosed cockpit with the hood sliding back, and enlarged dorsal fin, larger windscreen, and larger wheel spats, similar to those in the Ki-18 aeroplane offered to the Army Air Force. These changes resulted in a slight increase in weight, that of an empty aeroplane being 1,204 kg, and the take-off weight 1,659 kg.

The A5M2b version, also known as the "Type 96 carrier-borne naval fighter Model 2-2", failed to improve on earlier variants. This time the pilots complained about the performance. In addition, they were very much against the enclosed cockpit, introduced for the first time in a Japanese aeroplane, as they claimed that it would seriously limit visibility during combat, and for this reason it was often removed in operational units, and subsequently on the assembly line. The plant at Nagoya made 108 of the A5M2b version with enclosed cockpit, and a further 16 of these aircraft were assembled by the Dai-Nijuichi Kaigun Kokusho (21st Naval Aircraft Arsenal) at Omura which became an additional aircraft factory that supported production capabilities of the Nagoya plant. Aircraft with enclosed cockpits were manufactured at Omura after production at Nagoya ceased. In order to speed up deliveries of aircraft to the front line, production of the A5M2b version, but with open cockpit, continued later on both assembly lines.

At the same time two aircraft of an entirely experimental version were built, designated A5M3a, and sent for testing. A5M1 airframes were the basis, fitted with Hispano-Suiza 12Xcrs 12-cylinder liquid-cooled in-line V engines rated at 610 hp for take-off and 690 hp at 3,900 m. A 20 mm Hispano cannon was located between the cylinder banks,

*See Gloster Gladiator, Alex Crawford, MMP 2002.*

*A5M2b, 1/72 scale plans.*

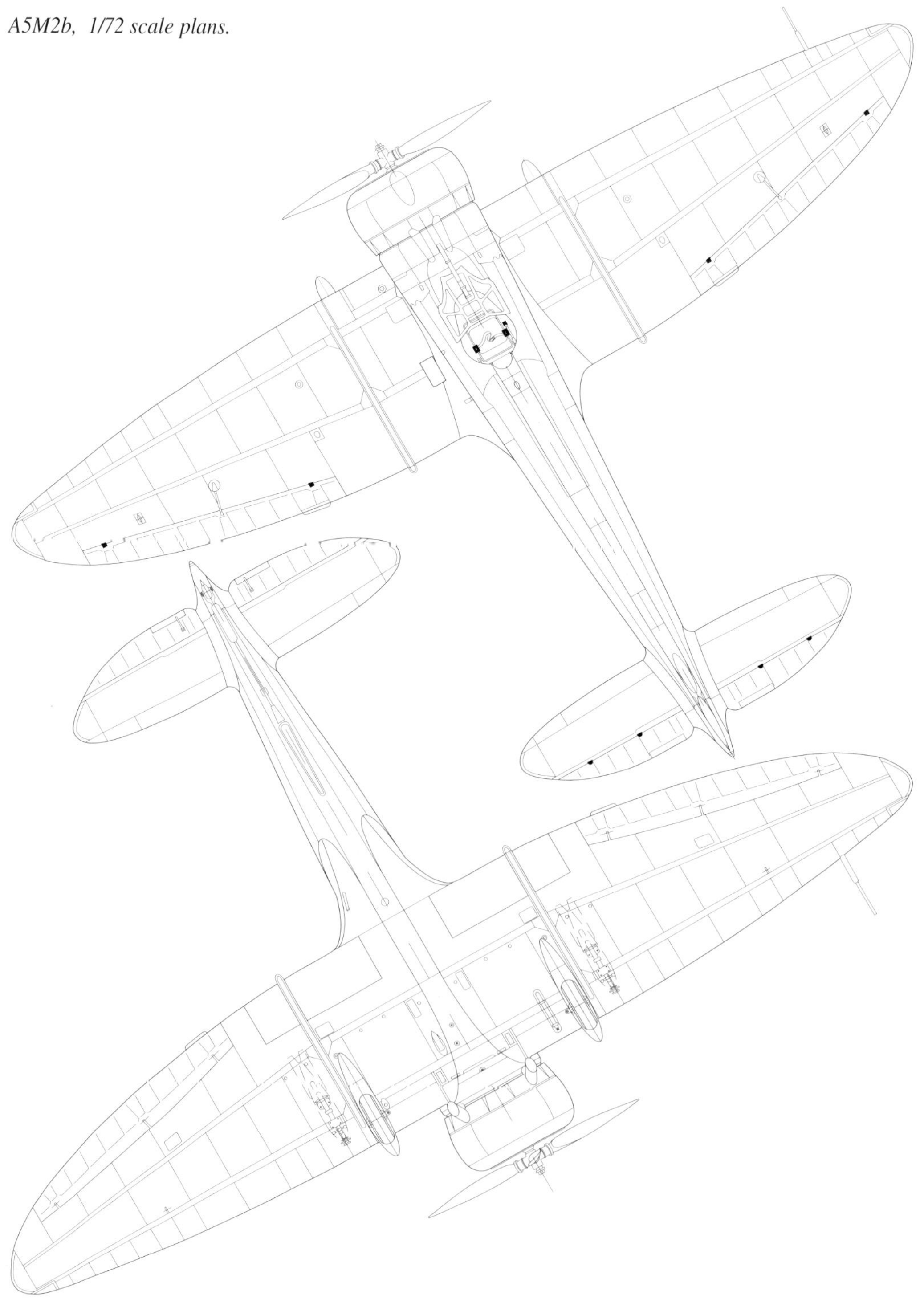

*A5M2b, 1/72 scale plans.*

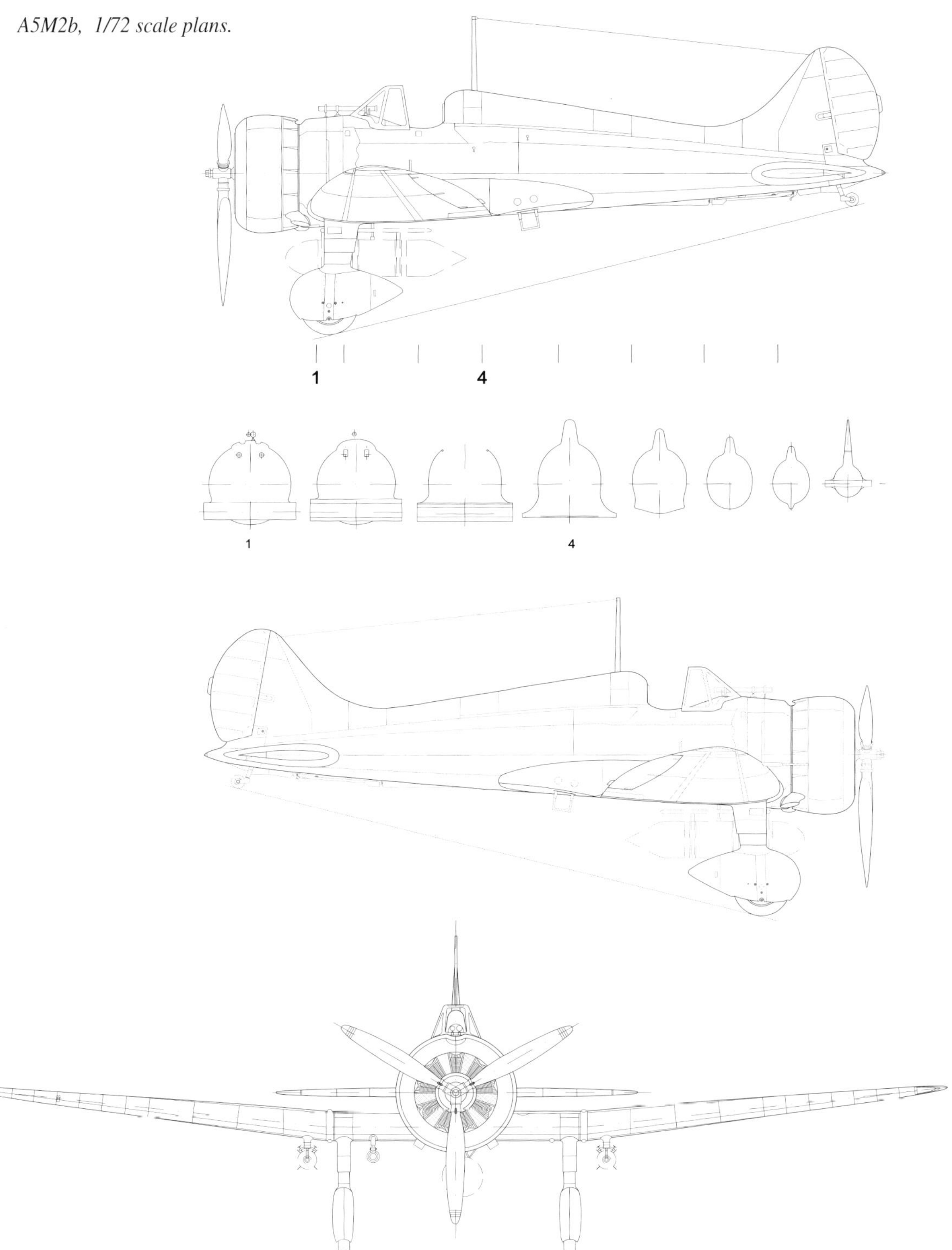

*A5M2b with closed canopy
1/72 scale plans.*

*A5M2b, field mod-
ificatin of the canopy
1/72 scale plan (side
view).*

firing through the propeller hub. Trials of that cannon were the main reason behind the development of the experimental A5M3a.

In April 1938 the Japanese were defeated at Taierchwang. Regular Chinese forces and partisans led by General Li Tsung-jen, their number probably exceeding 200,000, cut off and encircled 60,000 Japanese troops. Japanese forces broke through to the north, losing 20,000 killed and large amounts of materiel. The victory gave

*Above*:
A5M2b of 12 Kokutai.

*Left*:
A5M2bs of 13 Kokutai in flight over China.

a sudden boost to Chinese morale, but had no major effect on subsequent events. The Japanese soon regrouped and renewed their attacks. The line of the Japanese advance turned north, going around Hankow, but the old Chinese capital remained the main target of the Imperial Naval Aviation, its sky witnessing many major air combats that continued until the fall of the city on 25 October 1938.
The largest air battle of the Chinese-Japanese conflict

A5M4 with its pilot.

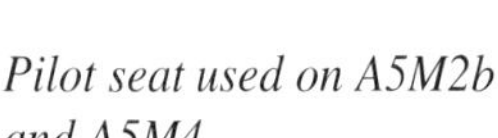

*Pilot seat used on A5M2b and A5M4.*

*Below:*
*A shotai of the 12 Kokutai in flight. "3-108" is the aircraft was flown by PO1c Kyosaku Aoki.*

took place over Hankow on 25 April 1938. The Chinese concentrated large fighter forces in the air bases around the city, waiting for an opportunity to counter attack. The Japanese knew these plans of the Chinese and, in order to outwit them, sent a formation of 18 Mitsubishi G3M2 bombers from the 13th Kokutai, escorted by 27 A5M fighters from the 12th Kokutai, led by Lt. Com. Yasuna Ozono. When the Japanese force arrived over Hankow, 78 Chinese I-152 and I-16 aircraft took off to intercept. During a 30-minute combat no less than 40 Chinese fighters were downed for the loss of only two A5M fighters and two G3M2 bombers. The success was achieved mainly thanks to the fact that the Japanese were opposed by pilots poorly trained and inexperienced in air combat. In spite of the great success, the Japanese knew from the experience of previous months that the Chinese fighter force at Hankow would be re-established, so on 31 May they organised another action against the Chinese force defending Hankow. 11 A5M aircraft of the 12th Kokutai and 24 from the 13th Kokutai escorted 18 G3M2 bombers over Hankow. Poor visibility in the attack area resulted in the 13th Kokutai failing to meet the enemy, but the A5Ms of the 12th Kokutai fought an epic battle against the 50 fighters defending the city. Eventually the Chinese lost 18 aircraft, including a Bellanca 28-90, the Chinese using the type as fighters.

After Anking was captured on 12 June 1938 and the newly formed 15th Kokutai was sent there, Japanese forces continued the attack up the Yangtze river, towards Wuhang. At that time the Chinese air units unexpectedly intensified their activities, and organised an attack of 49 bombers against Japanese ships on the river and against the front-line Japanese troops. Until the arrival of the 15th Kokutai to

Anking on 10 July, there were too few A5M aircraft in the area to provide proper defence. Their main task was to escort bombers over Hankow, Wuchang and Nanchang, and only a few times were they used to intercept Chinese attacks. A total of some 50 such attacks were made between 14 June and 28 July 1938. In July the scale of Chinese operations significantly decreased. There were only sporadic encounters between A5Ms escorting bombers over Nanchang and the defence. Then on 4 July the Chinese scrambled 65 fighters against 23 A5M fighters and 26 G3M2 bombers, and over half of the Chinese aircraft were destroyed, resulting in further reduction of the enemy's resistance. One event of that month shocked Japan, when Lt. Com. Mochifumi Nangoh, an excellent, famous and decorated pilot,

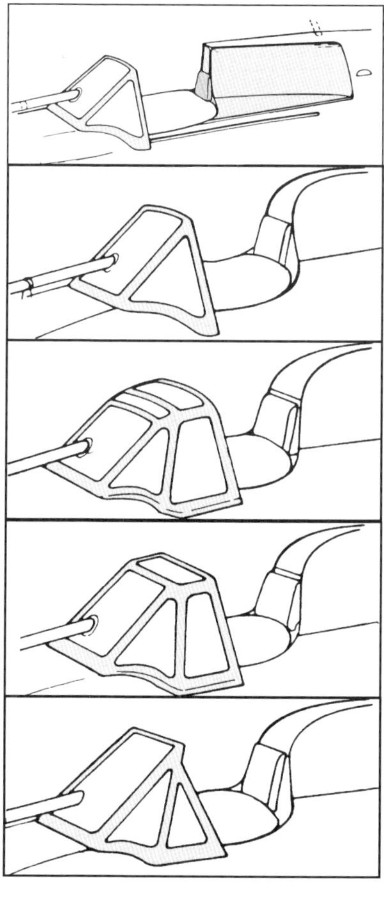

*Versions of the A5M2b & A5M4 canopies:*

*1. A5M2b (field modification)*
*2. A5M2b*
*3. A5M2 (last series)*
*4. A5M3b (late)*
*5. A5M4 (interim)*

*A5M2a of 15 Kokutai, photo was taken on 25 June 1938.*

*Three shots of A5M2b "9-122" of the 14th Kokutai, from the U.S. National Archives. This aircraft was captured by Chinese soldiers when it crash-landed at Weizhou (Wichow in some sources) Island in Southern China.*

was killed in combat. During a dog-fight with 11 Chinese fighters, Lieutenant Nangoh shot down a Gladiator. He then started to look around for another victim, but a burning Chinese fighter collided with his aeroplane. The wrecks, connected together, crashed into a lake. The Chinese fighter force revived by 3 August 1938, when over Hankow 21 A5M aircraft flying as escort to a bomber mission were

intercepted by some 50 Chinese fighters, of which no less than 27 were shot down for the loss of three Japanese aircraft. Major air battles were becoming rare, proving that the Chinese air force was losing

*Pair of A5M2bs of 12 Kokutai in flight, 1939.*

strength. Most Chinese combat aircraft in that area were destroyed on the ground, and those that survived in the air were chased away by the A5M fighters. From early August 1938 Mitsubishi A5M fighters claimed 330 air victories. The Chinese confirmed the loss of 1/3 of this number. The Japanese admitted losing some 30 A5M aircraft shot down in combat. However, in spite of the excellent characteristics of the Mitsubishi A5M fighter, the main reason behind this disproportionate kill ratio was the low level of training of the Chinese pilots and lack of aggression of most of them.

*Bottom:*
*A5M2a of 12 Kokutai, 1939.*

*Below:*
*Drawing of A5M4 canopy.*

# A5M3

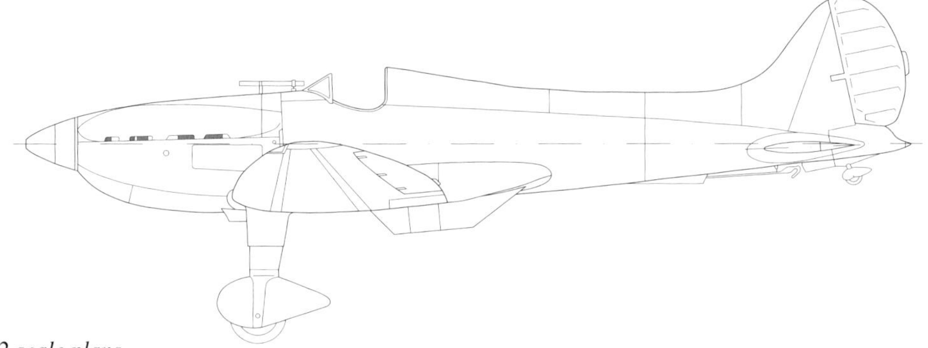

*A5M3 1/72 scale plans.*

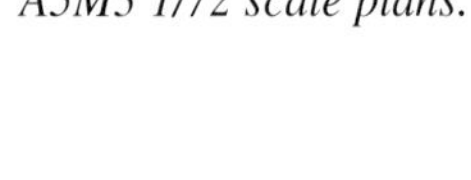

*A5M3 1/72 scale plans.*

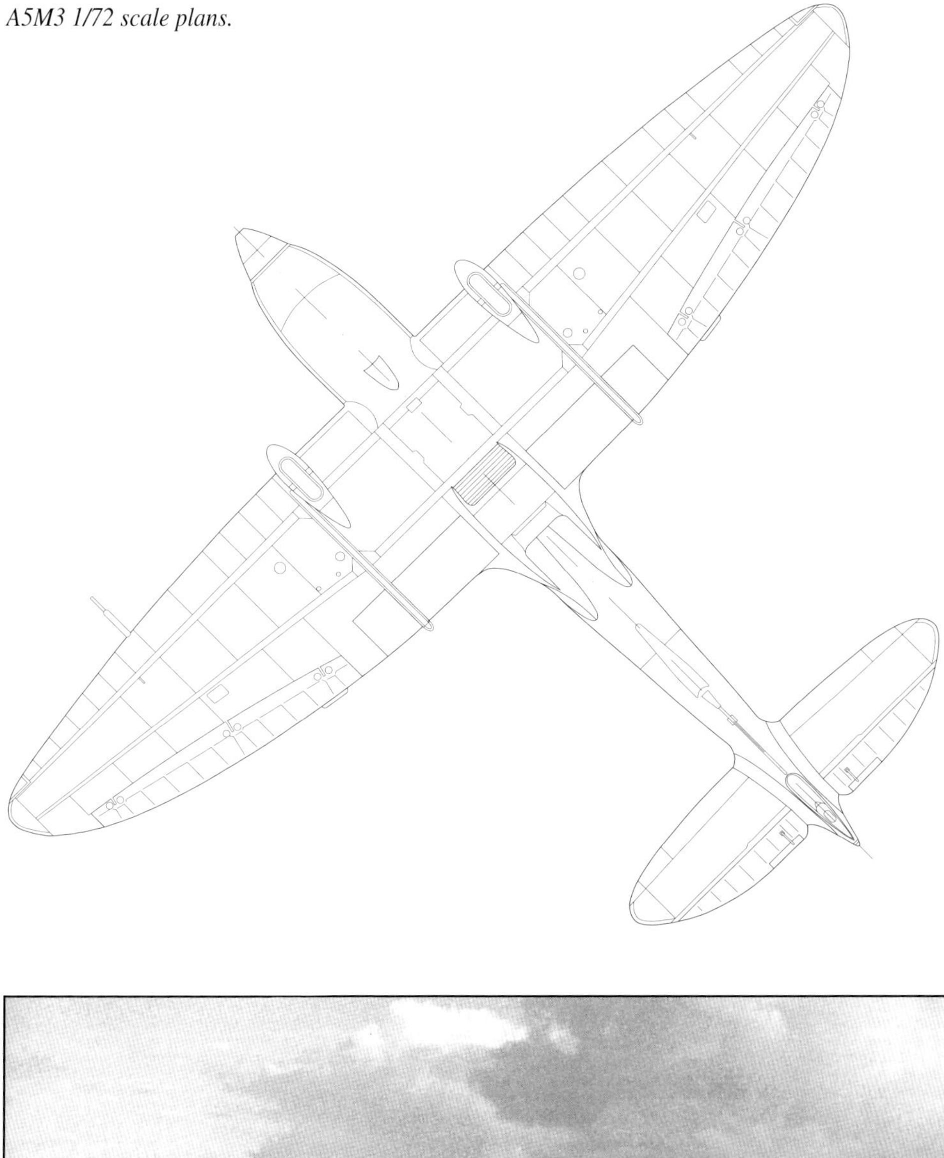

# A5M4

The Japanese were very satisfied with complete domination in the Chinese sky in their area of operations, that was significantly expanded after the introduction of the A5M, which forced the Chinese to move their air bases further inland. The new A5M4 version of the aeroplane was developed specially to disable the Chinese aircraft that remained outside the range of the A5M2.

The new version was externally almost identical to the last production A5M2b machines with the raised rear fuselage, reshaped windscreen, and with additional equipment. The A5M4, also designated "Type 96 carrier-borne naval fighter Model 2-4" was built in the largest numbers. Later on its designation was changed to A5M4 Model 24. It was powered by the Kotobuki 41 engine rated at 710 hp for take-off and 785 hp at 3,000 m. Apart from the changed engine, it also featured attachments for a 160 litre external drop tank that replaced the small (tear-drop shaped) tank, raising the maximum take-off weight to 1,707 kg, and the range and endurance to 648 km and 3 hours, respectively. Still later a

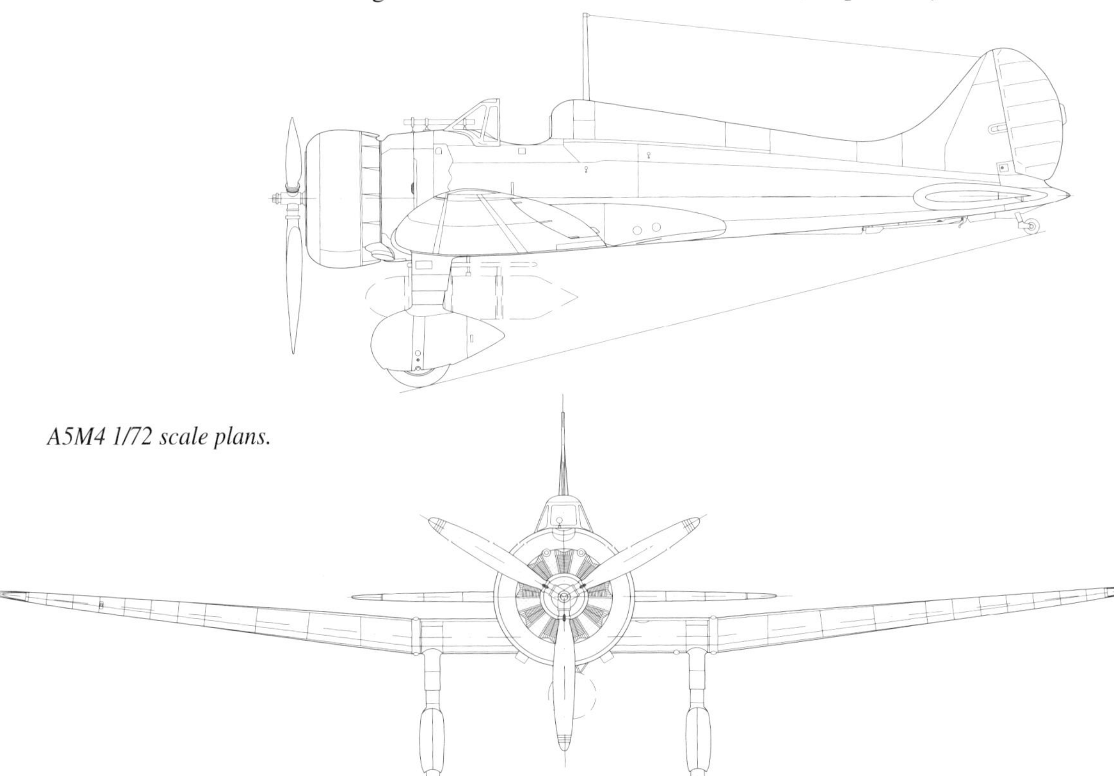

*A5M4 1/72 scale plans.*

*A5M4 1/72 scale plans.*

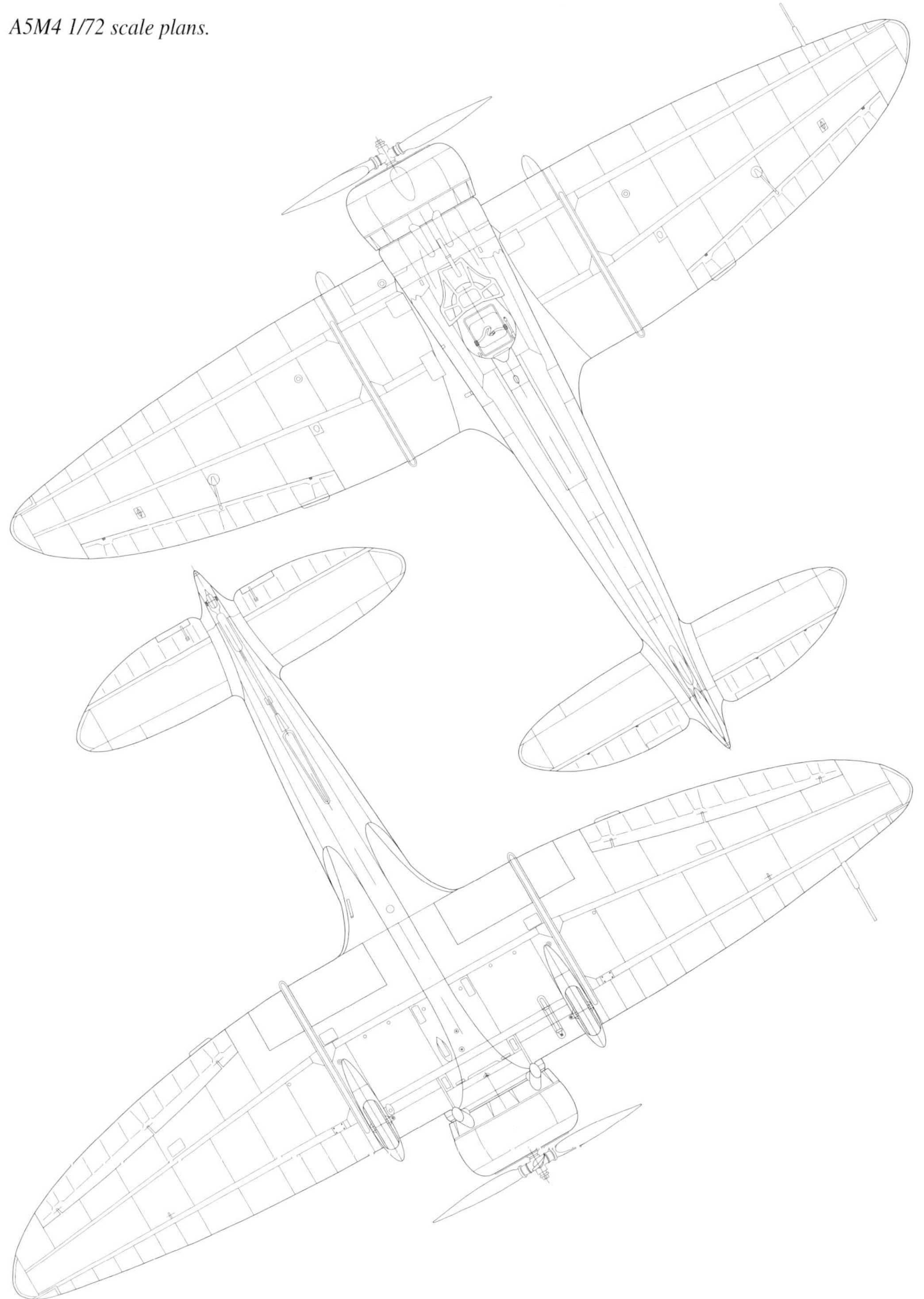

*A5M4 "W-101" piloted by Lt. Tomatsu YOKOYAMA takes off from the Soryu while on operations in the East China Sea, November 1938.*

**Below, right:**
*A5M4, "9-139", of 14th Kokutai flying over South China in 1940.*

**Below:**
*A5M4 of 14 Kokutai at Nanning Aerial Base in South China in the spring of 1940. The photo shows a shotai commander's plane parked in a protective revetment. The identification marking (red stripe with white outline) is shown right beside the oversea plane identification marking on the fuselage (the white fuselage band).*

210 litre tank was introduced and the aeroplane was upgraded to take either tank type. Even later the Kotobuki 41 Kai engine was introduced, the new variant receiving the designation A5M4 Model 34 with this power plant, which required slight alterations to the fuselage design. Both production variants were delivered to front line units until 1941. Production at the Nagoya plant and additionally at the 21st Naval Arsenal was later further expanded with the K. K. Watanabe Tekkosho company, although this delivered only a small part of the total number of air-

***Above:***
*Nakajima **Kotobuki 41**
9-cylinder air-cooled radial
engine.*

*Left:*
*A5M4 of 12 Kokutai.*

*Middle:*
*Another a5M4 of 12
Kokutai.*

***Bottom of the page:***
*A5M4 of an unknown unit.*

*A5M4 of an unknown unit.*

*A5M4, training version, Kasumigaura Kokutai at Omura, 1943.*

craft. During 1938-1940 the 21st Naval Aircraft Arsenal at Omura built 161 A5M2 and A5M4 aircraft, while Watanabe Tekkosho built just 39 A5M4 aircraft between 1939 and 1941.

During 1939 the A5M aircraft had very few opportunities to participate in air combat. Their activity was mostly in assault missions and patrolling Japanese bases. The A5Ms (16) of the aircraft carrier Akaga which arrived in the South China Sea area in early 1939 as replacement for the aircraft carrier Kaga, the latter going back to Japan for a major overhaul, had little to do. They supported ground forces in the absence of air combat. The Chinese skies of 1939 did not offer many opportunities for chasing the enemy like those at the beginning of the conflict, but there were incidents that for the most part proved the great potential of the A5M4. With the capture of Hankow, the Japanese established an important airfield in its vicinity, code-named "W" air base. For a long time Chinese activity in the air was almost negligible. On 3 October 1939 high ranking Japanese officers gathered at the "W" base awaiting new aircraft to be delivered from Japan. Suddenly, without warning, 8 Chinese SB bombers appeared over the base at an altitude of 7,000 m, and dropped some 50 bombs. Seven high ranking Japanese officers were killed, and 12 more, including Vice Admiral Nishizo Tsukahara, commanding the 1st Rengo Kokutai (1st Joint Air Corps), were

seriously wounded. Many aircraft were destroyed on the ground, including a few A5Ms. Eleven days later the "W" air base. was subject to a similar attack. Twenty Chinese SB bombers destroyed some 40 Navy aircraft and 20 Army ones. The last major air battles took place over Liuchow and Kweilin on 30 December 1939 and 10 January 1940. The first of this

involved 13 A5Ms intercepted by 20 Chinese I-152 and I-16 fighters, of which 14 were shot down for the loss of a single A5M. During the second engagement 26 A5Ms of the 12th and 14th Kokutais fought a similar number of Chinese fighters, shooting down 13 of the latter for no loss.

Combats over China created seven aces flying the A5M, and of these Lieutenant Tetsuzoh Iwamoto of the 12th Kokutai scored most victories. During his first combat, on 25 February 1938 over Nanchang, he claimed five Chinese fighters, and by the time he was recalled to Japan he had scored 14 kills in 82 combat sorties. Two

*Top of the page:*
*A5M4s in a line.*

***Above:***
*Photo of the aircraft and the pilots of the Soryu Kokutai.*

***Left:***
*A5M4. Note access grips.*

pilots achieved 13 victories: Warrant Officer Kiyozumi Koga and Warrant Officer Toshio Kuroiwa of the 13th and 12th Kokutai Koga opened his score during the attack at Nanking on 19 September 1937, and was posted back to Japan in December of that year. Kuroiwa scored most of his victories during

*Above:*
*A5M4 of Chitose Kokutai at Kwajalein Island, December 1941*

*Right:*
*Bomb loading on A5M4.*

*Below:*
*A5M2 of 14 Kokutai, 1938.*

three months in the spring of 1938, and the next year he left the Imperial Naval Aviation to fly in Japanese air lines. Twelve victories were scored by Sergeant Kuniyoshi Tanaka of the 13th Kokutai, who claimed his first two kills over Nanchang on 9 December 1937. Sergeant Sadaaki Akamatsu and Lieutenant Motonari

*A5M4s, personal aircraft of Suho and Kofukuda*

Suhoh scored 11 victories each, and the seventh ranking A5M ace, Sergeant Momoto Matsumura, was credited with 10 victories. During large scale preparations for the war which the Japanese government sought, the Imperial Navy started to hand over its air operations to the Army Air Force, and in September 1941 only 17 of its bombers and 3 seaplanes were still in the Chinese theatre. Four more Kokutais that had been formed were equipped

*Left:*
*A5M4. Photo was taken from right behind the plane and is very useful for seeing the cross section shape of the windshield and the dorsal fin.*

*Below:*
*A5M4 as a training aircraft, note the main gear covers partially removed.*

solely with A5M4 aircraft. Two of these were briefly engaged in fighting in China. These were the Genzan Kokutai and the 1st Kokutai. In November 1940 the Genzan Kokutai formed in Korea with 24 A5M4 fighters and 36 G3M bombers, being moved to Hankow in April 1941. It was employed there against ground targets and on base protection duties for four months, until another transfer back to Korea, where its fighter formation would wait until the arrival of the new Mitsubishi A6M Reisen fighters in April 1942. The 1st Kokutai was formed in April 1941 with similar aircraft numbers to the Genzan Kokutai, and in a similar manner it was deployed to Hankow, where it acted as the air defence until September 1941, when the A5M4s were transferred to the 3rd Kokutai and Tainang Kokutai being formed on Formosa. The next two units included the Chitose Kokutai, formed at Chi-

tose on Hokkaido in October 1939 with 36 A5M4s and several G3M bombers. It remained at the home base until deployed to the Marshall Islands in November 1941. The last of these units was the 3rd Kokutai, initially formed as a bomber unit, but re-formed in September 1941 as a pure fighter outfit with a mixed composition of 12 A5M4 and 45 A6M2 aircraft. Retention of the old A5Ms was dictated by the fact that the 3rd Kokutai used these aircraft for base protection and training.

In November 1941, immediately before the outbreak of the Pacific War, a temporary fighter group was formed in Malaya, composed of 12 A5M4 and 27 A6M2 fighters plus 6 Mitsubishi C5M1 reconnaissance aircraft, later incorporated into the 22nd Koku Sentai. When the war broke out, A5M aircraft still equipped fighter units on the aircraft carriers Hosho and Ryujo and on the light carriers Zuiho and Shoho. These joined the Imperial Japanese Navy in December 1940 and December 1941 respectively, after conversion from the tankers Takasaki and Kenzaki. A5Ms also served in base defence units in the home islands at Sasebo, Omura, Ominato, and Takao. Lack of sufficient numbers of A6M Reisen fighters forced the Chitose Kokutai,

*A5M4 Claudes of 12 Kokutai.*

*A5M4s of an unknown unit waiting for the next mssion.*

*A5M4, engine overhaul.
Note the aileron actuating
arm.*

sent to the Marshall Islands a few weeks before the outbreak of war, to use A5M4s. In February 1942 the 4th Kokutai was formed, which included 13 A5M4 fighters and 27 bombers operating from Rabaul in New Britain. In April of that year, within the 1st Kokutai that had given away its fighter unit in September of the previous year, a new fighter group of 13 A5M4 aircraft was formed, to defend the Marshall Islands. The A5M4s of the unit were soon replaced by new A6M2 Reisen fighters as these became available. Similarly, in the 6th Kokutai, also established in April 1942, the 14 A5M4 aircraft were replaced by the new fighters. From the time of the Pearl Harbor attack, the A5M had little time left as a front line carrier-borne fighter, but before the type was finally withdrawn, it participated in some final fights. Several hundred A5Ms were still in the Navy inventory, over a half used for training, and some 100 to 200 remained in the front line awaiting replacement by the A6M Reisen.

*A5M4. Photo was taken

in January 1942.*

As mentioned before, 36 A5M4 aircraft of the Chitose Kokutai were soon moved to the Marshall Islands (24 to Luot and 12 to Taloa). Thirteen A5M4s of the newly formed fighter unit of the 1st Kokutai were sent to Palau, and soon afterwards they entered combat, but the first of these that participated in fighting took off from the aircraft carrier Ryujo on 8 December. A group of nine A5Ms, escorting Nakajima B5N bombers heading to Davao in Mindanao, was led by Lieutenant Takahide Aioi. A5M aircraft based on the aircraft carrier Ryujo continued attacks against Davao until the town was occupied by the Japanese in late December 1941, and only one A5M was lost during these actions. It was shot down by AA fire, and its pilot Sergeant Hiroshi Kawanishi baled out after seeing his aeroplane was on fire. Later on, the aircraft carrier Ryujo was moved to support operations in Malaya, and before that, in January 1942, it participated in the invasion of the Dutch East Indies. Then it was earmarked for operations in the Bay of Bengal area, until sent back to Japan, where it arrived on 23 April 1942. It was there that all the A5M aircraft were replaced by the new A6M fighters.

On 1 February 1942 the Japanese forces in the Marshall Islands were attacked by the US Navy Task Force that consisted, among others, of the aircraft carriers Enterprise and Yorktown. The A5M2 aircraft from Luot and Taloa managed to intercept US aircraft from the Enterprise, claiming destruction of 17. The A5Ms split among Luot, Taloa, and Wake did not participate in combat again, and according to Navy reports 19 of these aircraft remained in operational service until 1 April 1942 together with 9 A6M aircraft, later replaced by more modern fighters. Thirteen 3rd Kokutai and Tainang Kokutai A5Ms delivered to Rabaul performed combat missions as night fighters, using ground searchlights. The first successful action took place on 11 February 1942, when three Hudson bombers were destroyed. A day later the A5Ms were included in the newly formed 4th Kokutai, soon replaced by the more modern A6Ms. The last air combat of an A5M took place on 7 May 1942. On that day at 9.00 the aircraft carrier Shoho was attacked by US aeroplanes that launched no less than seven torpedoes and 13 bombs. After some 20 minutes the Japanese aircraft carrier sank. Two A5M and four A6M fighters that managed to get airborne before the sinking, led by Lieutenant Kenjiroh Nohtomi, destroyed 3 US aircraft. Although the Japanese aircraft suffered no losses in combat, they were forced to ditch as their aircraft carrier had been sunk, and one managed to land at a nearby island.

A5M aircraft continued in service as advanced trainers, and during the final, crucial, period for aircraft to defend the Japanese Islands they resumed service as interceptor fighters.

# A5M4-K

In early 1940 production of single-seat A5M4 Model 24 and A5M4 Model 34 versions was discontinued by the Nagoya plant after 782 aircraft of all series were manufactured. But the Dai-Nijuichi Kaigun Kokusho, after termination of production and delivery of the 161st A5M4 fighter, continued production of the A5M4-K two-seater

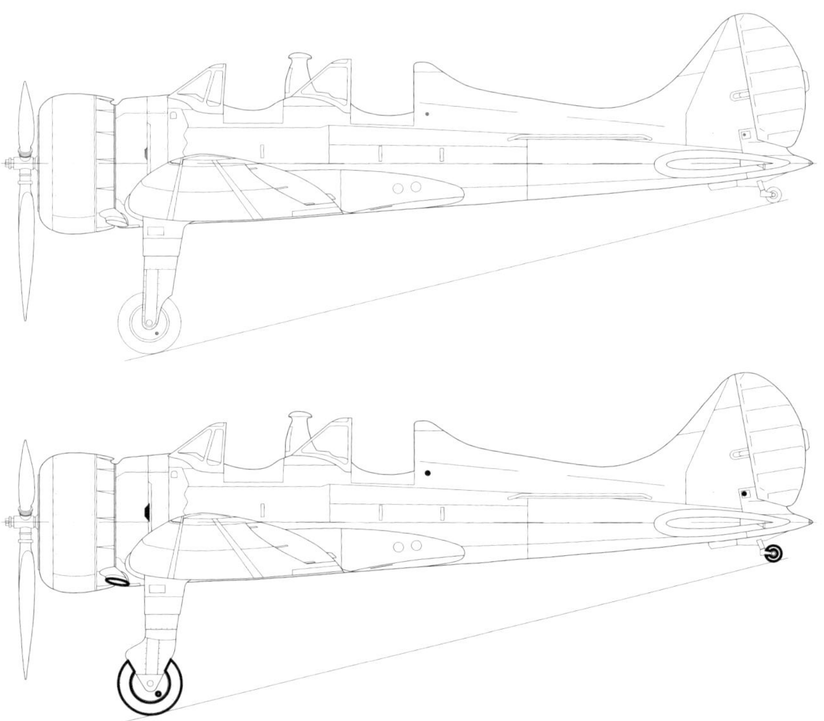

*A5M4-ks side views 1/72 scale plans.*

trainer, powered by Kotobuki 41 or similar Kotobuki 41 Kai engine. This version was developed by the Arsenal at Omura against the 15 Shi specification formulated by the Kaigun Koku Hombu in 1941. The size of the A5M4-K trainer remained the same as the fighter, but the firewall was repositioned, the engine mount shortened, the cockpit moved slightly forward, and a rear cockpit for the instructor was located over the wing trailing edge. A turnover structure was fitted aft of the forward cockpit, and in order to improve spin recovery characteristics, stabilisers were introduced on the rear fuselage sides. Wheel spats were also removed.

Production of the A5M4-K continued at the Arsenal from 1942 until 1944. 103 machines of the type were manufactured. Several of these remained in service as trainers until the end of the war, and were even used, together with the single-seat variants, for Kamikaze attacks. This was the end of the career of an excellent aeroplane, that had ended the period of weakness of Japanese aviation and allowed it to achieve the same technological level as that of Western aircraft designs. The moment the war broke out in the Pacific, Allied intelligence gave the code-name Claude to all the versions of the A5M4 aeroplane, and reserved the name Sandy for the version with the W-shaped wing which, as we know now, never entered service as a combat aeroplane, only existing as a prototype and being destroyed during static trials. The following units used the A5M: aircraft carriers Akagi, Hosho, Kaga, Ryujo, Shoho, Soryu, Zuiho, and air corps 12, 13, 14, 15, Chitose, Oita, Ominato, Omura, Sasebo, Tainang and Yokosuka Kokutai,

*Left:*
*A5M4-k, October, 1944, of Air School Oita Kokutai.*

*Below:*
*A5M4-k, prototype, built in December 1942 by Sasebo Naval Arsenal.*

# Specifications:

Description: single-seat carrier-borne fighter (A5M1 to A5M4), single-seat land-based fighter (Ki-18 and Ki-33), two-seater fighter trainer (A5M4-K). All-metal construction with fabric covered ailerons and tail control surfaces.

Crew: pilot in an open cockpit (all versions except A5M2b Model 2-2, Ki-33 and A5M4-K). Pilot in an enclosed cockpit (A5M2b Model 2-2 and Ki-33). Pupil pilot and instructor in open cockpits (A5M4-K).

Power plant:

One Nakajima Kotobuki 5 9-cylinder air-cooled radial engine rated at 550 hp (404 kW) for take-off, 600 hp (441 kW) at 3,100 m, two-bladed variable pitch metal propeller, dia. 2.9 m, fuel tank capacity 200 litres (Ka-14 1st prototype and Ki-18),

One Nakajima Kotobuki 3 9-cylinder air-cooled radial engine rated at 640 hp (470 kW) for take-off, 715 hp (526 kW) at 2,800 m, two-bladed variable pitch metal propeller, dia. 2.69 m, (Ka-14 2nd prototype), three-bladed variable pitch metal propeller, dia. 2.900 m, fuel tank capacity 330 litres (A5M2b),

One Nakajima Hikari 1 9-cylinder air-cooled radial engine rated at 700 hp (515 kW) for take-off, 800 hp (588 kW) at 3,500 m, two-bladed variable pitch metal propeller, dia. 2.69 m (Ka-14 3rd, 4th and 5th prototypes),

One Nakajima Kotobuki 2 Kai 1 9-cylinder air-cooled radial engine

*A5M4-k of an unknown Air School.*

rated at 580 hp (426 kW) for take-off, 630 hp (463 kW) at 1,500 m, two-bladed variable pitch metal propeller, dia. 2.69 m, fuel tank capacity 330 litres (A5M1),

One Nakajima Kotobuki 2 Kai 3b 9-cylinder air-cooled radial engine rated at 610 hp (448 kW) for take-off, 690 hp (507 kW) at 3,250 m, three-bladed variable pitch metal propeller, dia. 2.98 m, fuel tank capacity 330 litres (A5M2a),

One Hispano-Suiza 12Xcrs 12-cylinder liquid-cooled V in-line engine rated at 610 hp (448 kW) for take-off, 690 hp (507 kW) at 3,900 m, three-bladed variable pitch metal propeller, dia. 2.9 m (A5M3a),

One Nakajima Kotobuki 41 or 41 Kai 9-cylinder air-cooled radial engine rated at 710 hp (522 kW) for take-off, 785 hp (577 kW) at 3,000 m, three-bladed variable pitch metal propeller, dia. 2.98 m, fuel tank capacity 330 litres + additional 160 litre drop fuel tank (A5M4 and A5M4-K)

One Mitsubishi Kinsei A-8 or A-9 14-cylinder air-cooled radial engine, three-bladed variable pitch metal propeller (experimental installation in one Ka-14 prototype),

One Nakajima Ha-1b 9-cylinder air-cooled radial engine rated at 710 hp (522 kW) for take-off, 745 hp (548 kW) at 3,700 m, two-bladed variable pitch metal propeller, dia. 3.06 m (Ki-33),

Armament:

Two 0.303 in. Type 89 machine guns in the upper fuselage (all versions except as mentioned in the text),

One 20 mm Hispano cannon (A5M3a),

External stores: two 30 kg bombs (A5M2b and A5M4) or one 160 litre drop fuel tank (A5M4),

# Technical Data

| Version | Ka-14 1st prototype | A5M1 | A5M2a | A5M2b | A5M3a | A5M4 | A5M4-K | Ki-18 |
|---|---|---|---|---|---|---|---|---|
| **Dimensions:** | | | | | | | | |
| Wing span (m) | 11.000 | 11.00 | 11.00 | 11.00 | 11.00 | 11.00 | 11.00 | 11.00 |
| Length (m) | 7.670 | 7.710 | 7.545 | 7.565 | 8.377 | 7.565 | 7.655 | 7.655 |
| Height (m) | 3.265 | 3.200 | 3.200 | 3.270 | 3.095 | 3.237 | 3.237 | 3.150 |
| Wing area (m²) | 17.80 | 17.80 | 17.80 | 17.80 | 17.80 | 17.80 | 17.80 | 16.00 |
| **Weights (kg):** | | | | | | | | |
| Empty weight | 1,040 | 1,075 | 1,184 | 1,234 | | 1,216 | 1,263 | 1,110 |
| Take-off weight | 1,373 | 1,500 | 1,609 | 1,697 | | 1,671 | 1,707 | 1,422 |
| Useful load | 333 | 425 | 425 | 463 | | 455 | 444 | 312 |
| Wing loading (kg/m²) | 77.13 | 84.27 | 90.39 | 95.34 | | 93.88 | 95.90 | 88.87 |
| Power loading (kg/hp) | 2.50 | 2.59 | 2.64 | 2.65 | | 2.35 | 2.40 | 2.58 |
| **Performance:** | | | | | | | | |
| Maximum speed (km/h) | 450 | 406 | 426 | | | 435 | 442 | 445 |
| at an altitude of (m) | 3,200 | 2,100 | 3,090 | | | 3,000 | 3,160 | 3,050 |
| Cruising speed (km/h) | | | 347 | | | 395 | | |
| at an altitude of (m) | | | 3,000 | | | 3,000 | | |
| Landing speed (km/h) | | | | | | 113 | | |
| Time to climb | 5'54" | 8'30" | 7'59" | | | 3'35" | | 6'26" |
| to altitude of (m) | 5,000 | 5,000 | 5,000 | | | 3,000 | | 5,000 |
| Ceiling (m) | 9,450 | 9,450 | | | | 9,800 | 9,830 | |
| Range (km) | | 705 | 705 | | | 1,200 | | |
| Take-off run (m) | | | | | | 220 | | |
| Landing run (m) | | | | | | 420 | | |
| Endurance (h) | | | | 2 | | 4 | | |

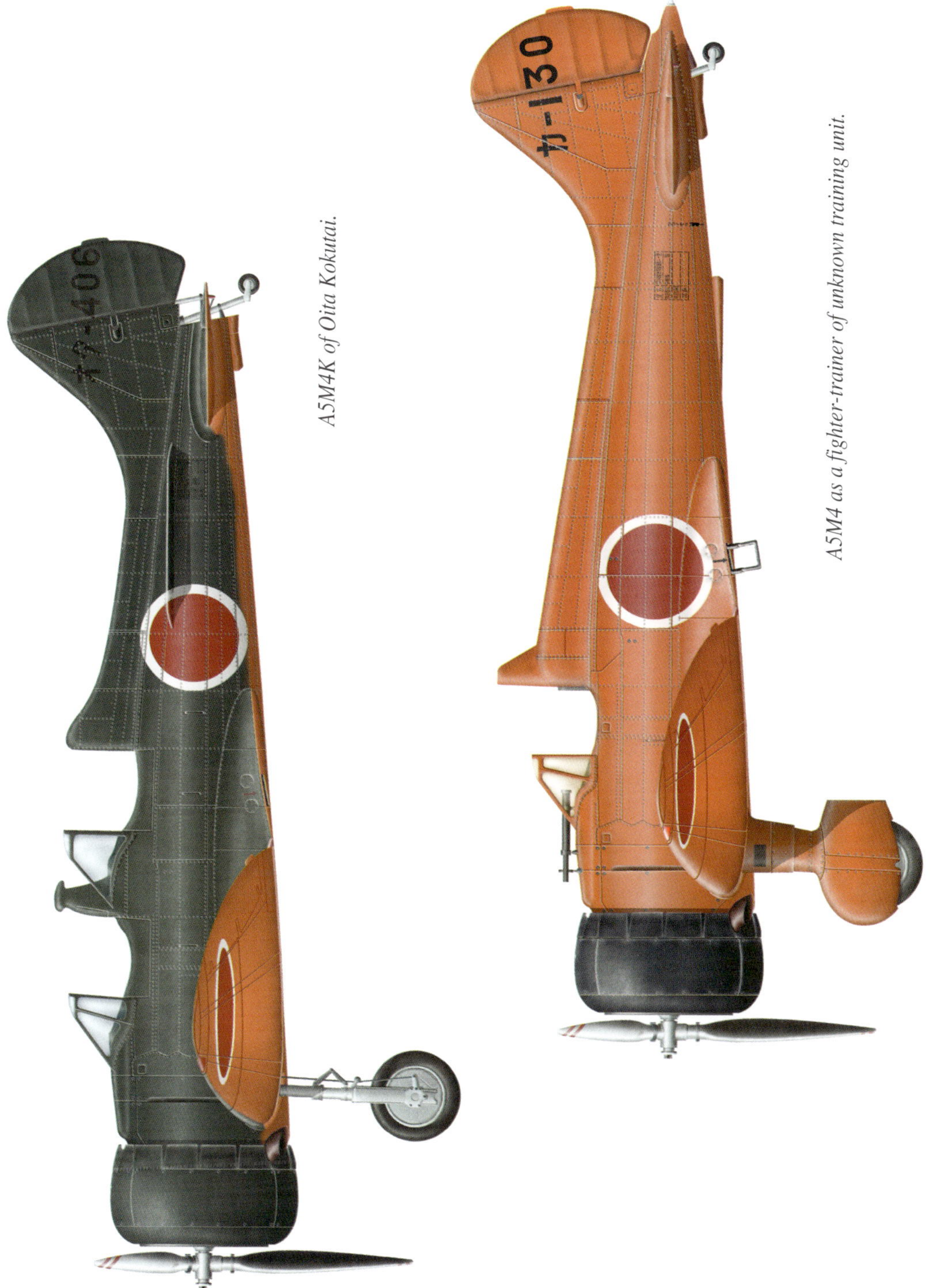

A5M4K of Oita Kokutai.

A5M4 as a fighter-trainer of unknown training unit.

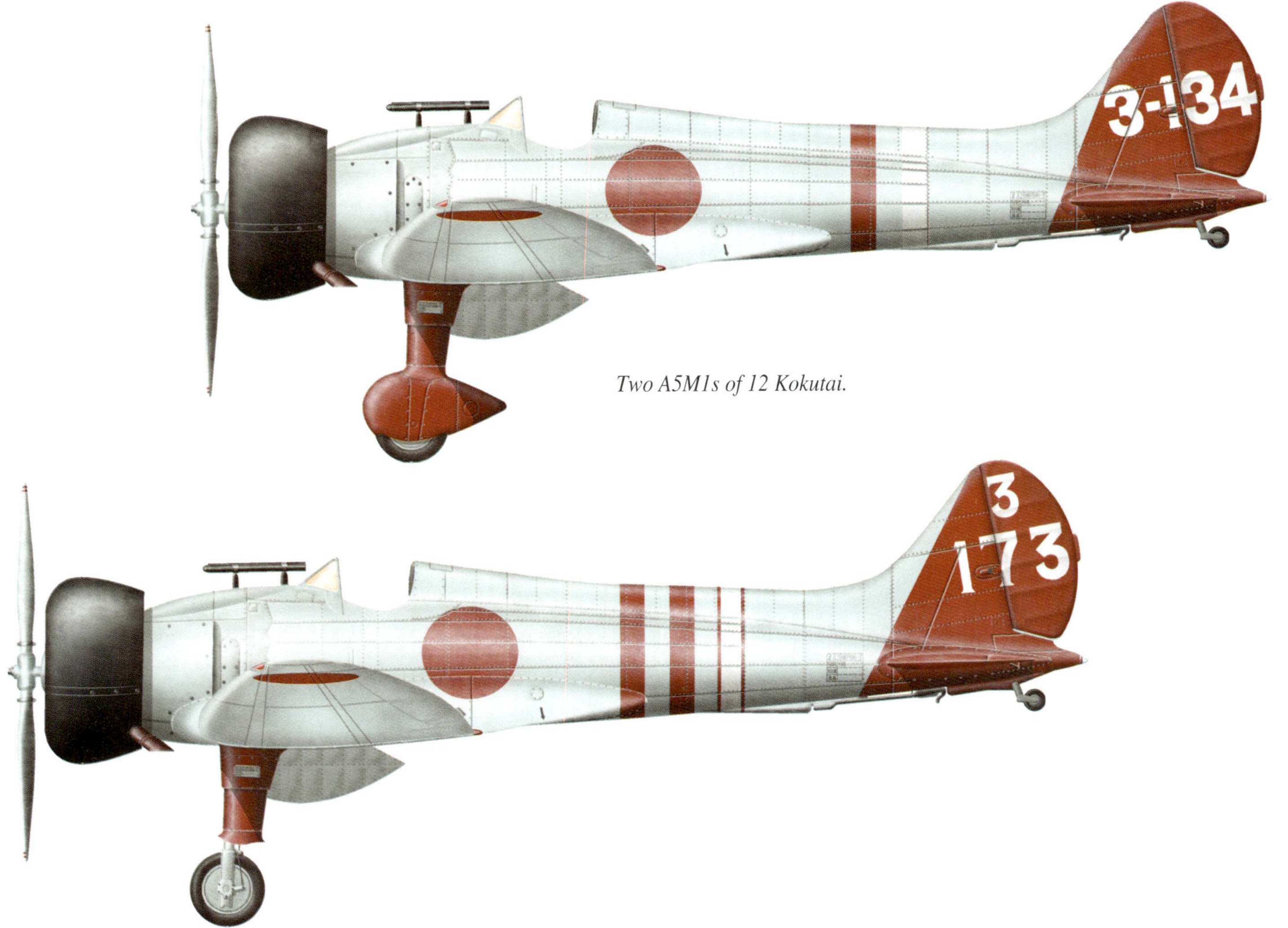

*Two A5M1s of 12 Kokutai.*

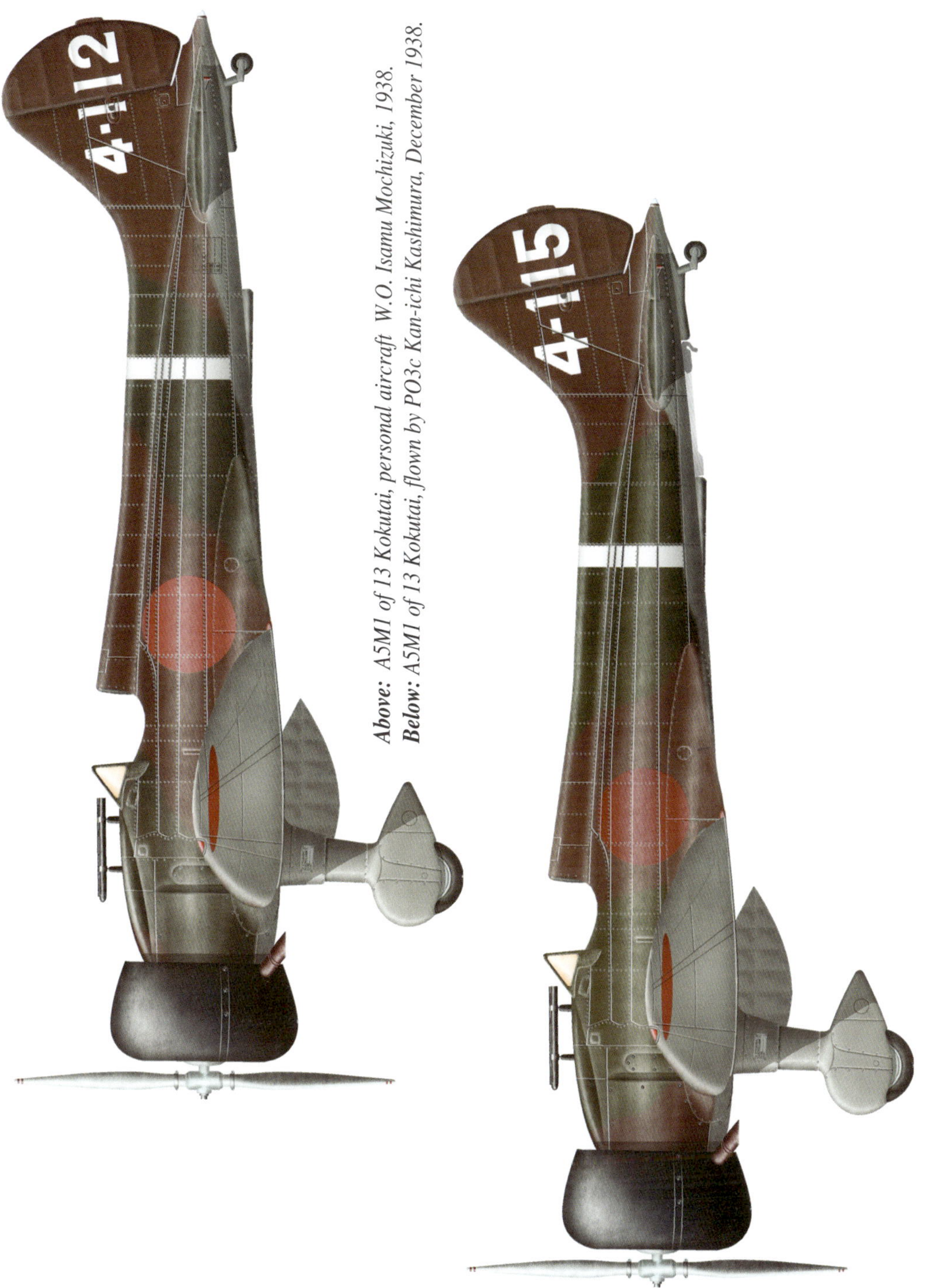

**Above:** *A5M1 of 13 Kokutai, personal aircraft W.O. Isamu Mochizuki, 1938.*
**Below:** *A5M1 of 13 Kokutai, flown by PO3c Kan-ichi Kashimura, December 1938.*

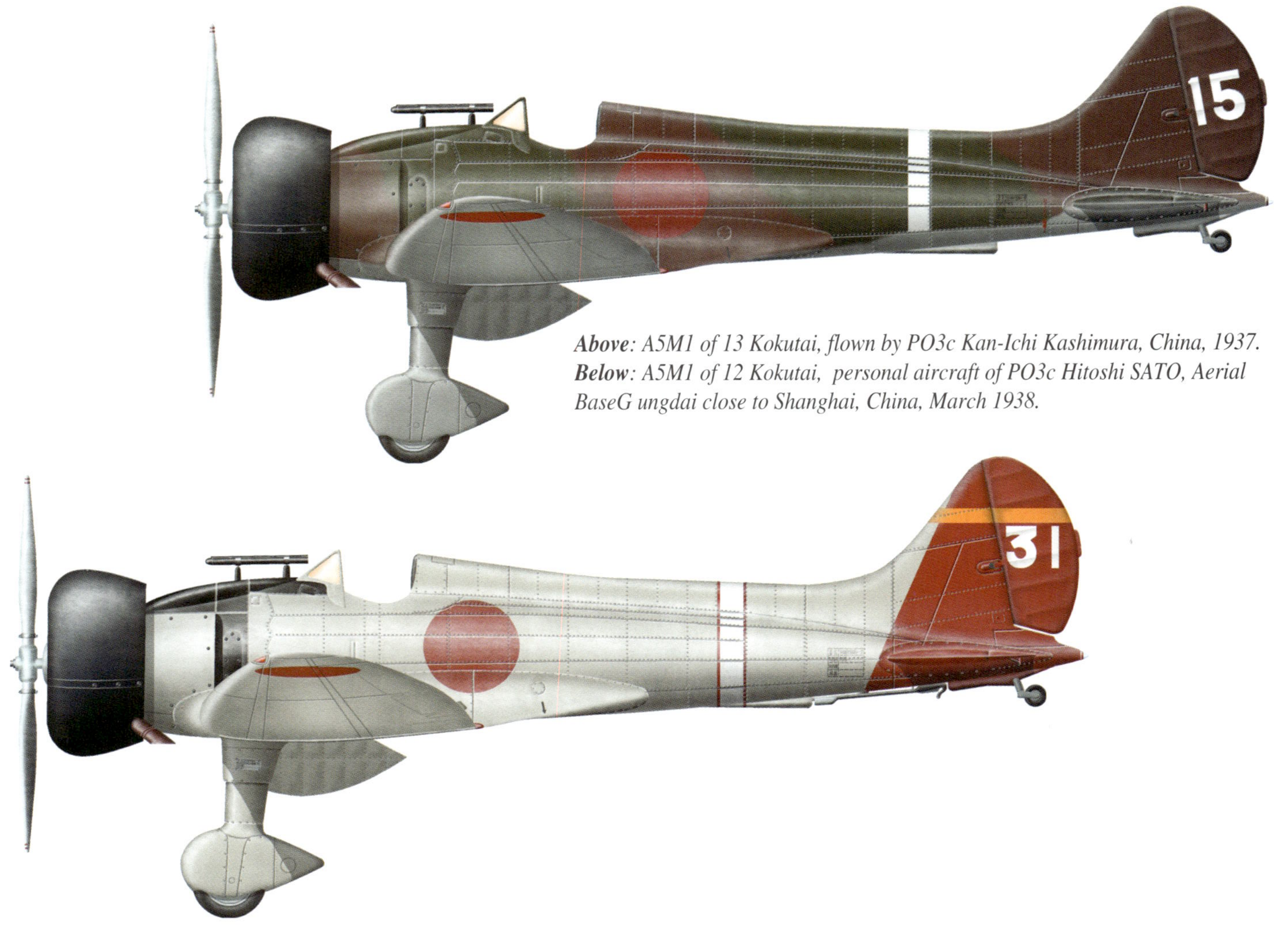

**Above**: A5M1 of 13 Kokutai, flown by PO3c Kan-Ichi Kashimura, China, 1937.
**Below**: A5M1 of 12 Kokutai, personal aircraft of PO3c Hitoshi SATO, Aerial BaseG ungdai close to Shanghai, China, March 1938.

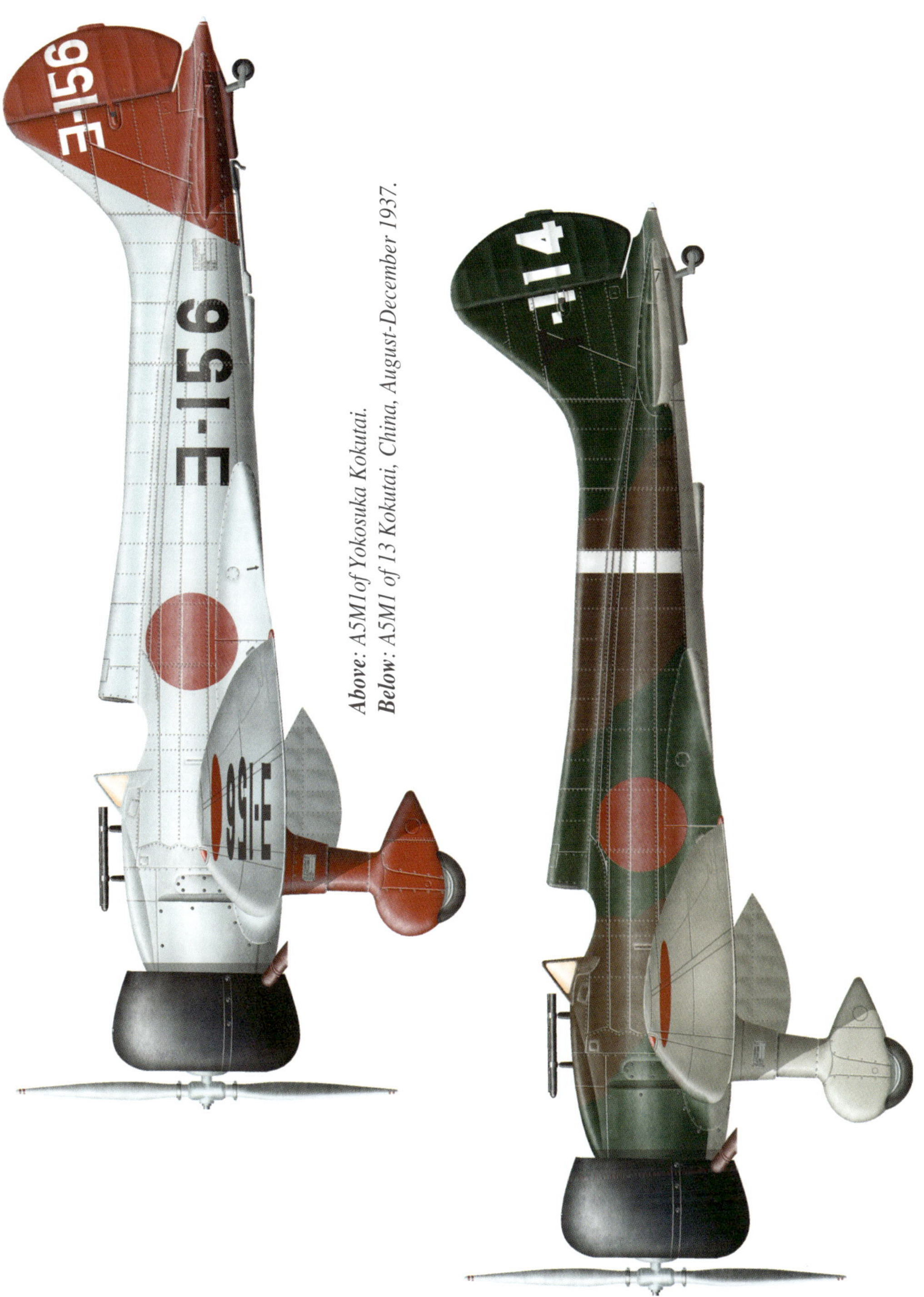

*Above: A5M1 of Yokosuka Kokutai.*
*Below: A5M1 of 13 Kokutai, China, August-December 1937.*

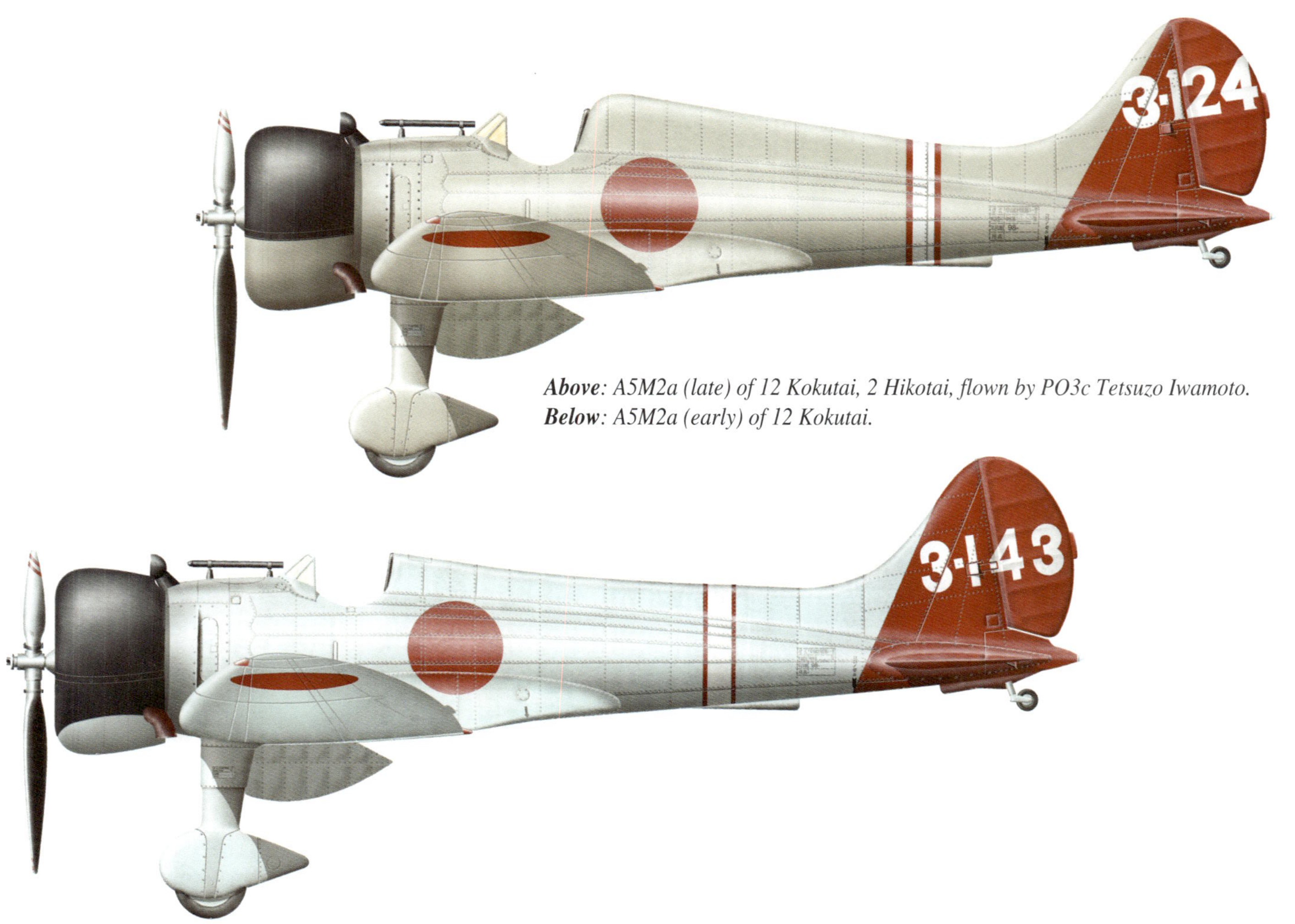

*Above*: A5M2a (late) of 12 Kokutai, 2 Hikotai, flown by PO3c Tetsuzo Iwamoto.
*Below*: A5M2a (early) of 12 Kokutai.

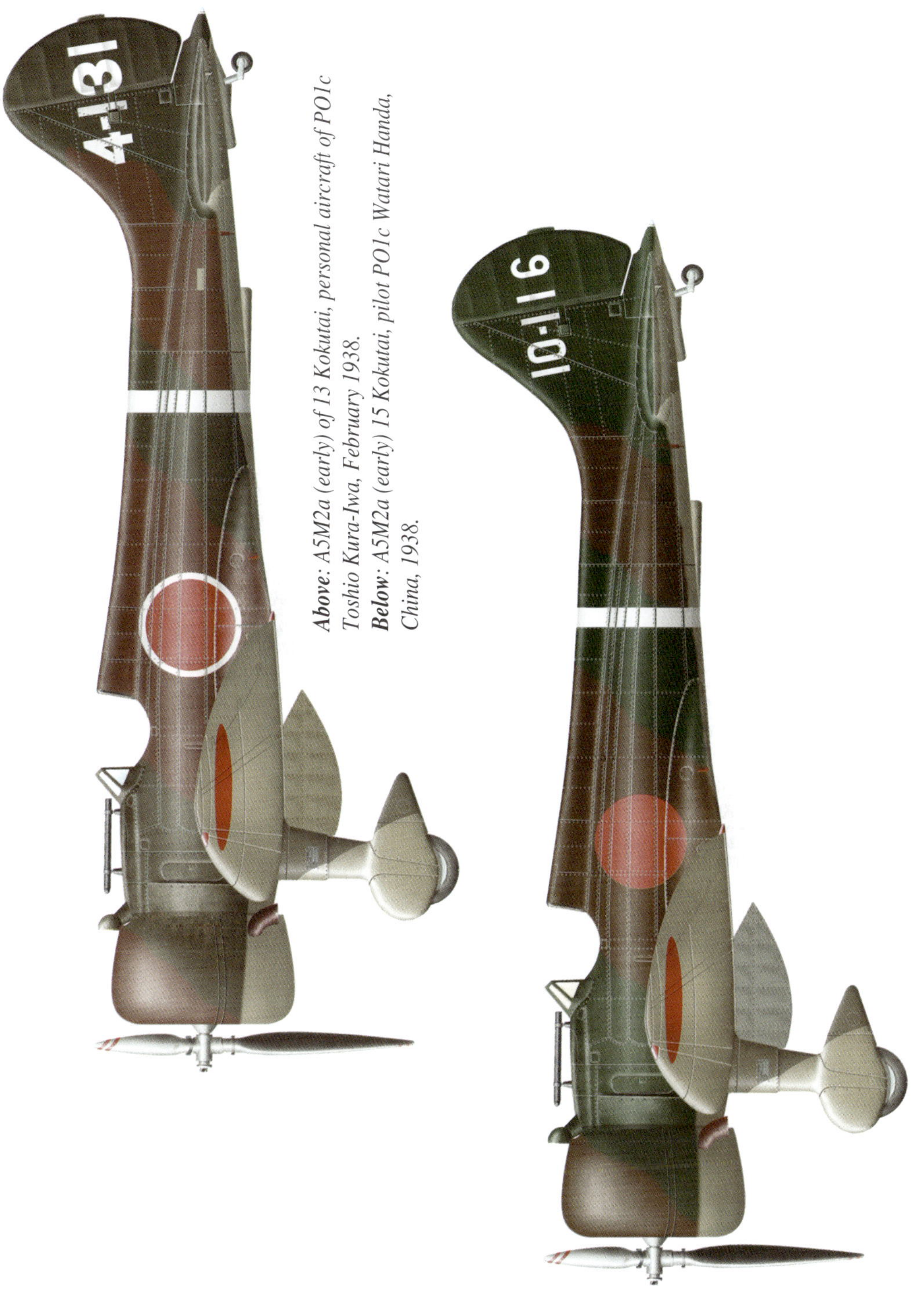



**Above**: *A5M2a (early) of 13 Kokutai, personal aircraft of PO1c Toshio Kura-Iwa, February 1938.*
**Below**: *A5M2a (early) 15 Kokutai, pilot PO1c Watari Handa, China, 1938.*

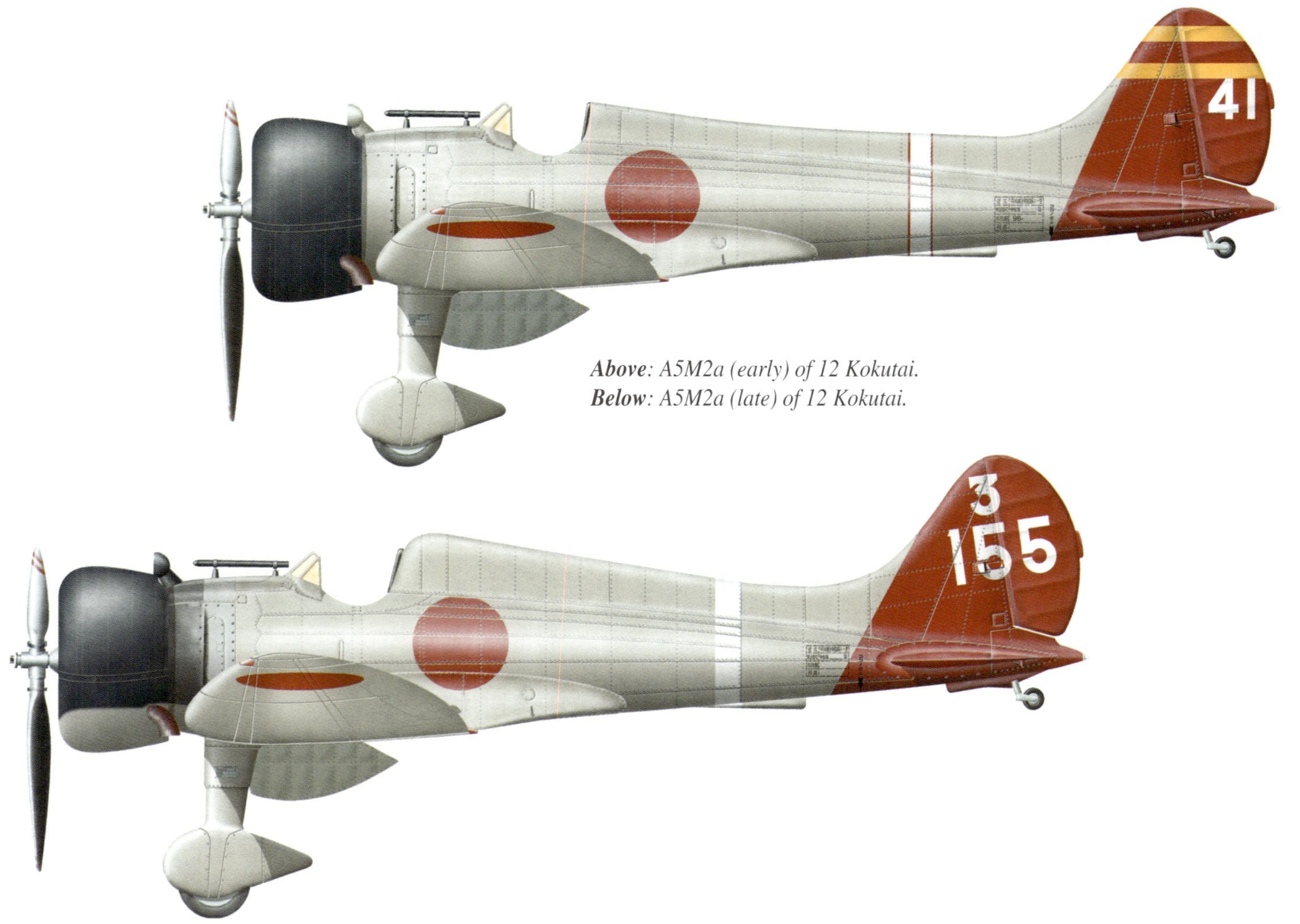

*Above*: A5M2a (early) of 12 Kokutai.
*Below*: A5M2a (late) of 12 Kokutai.

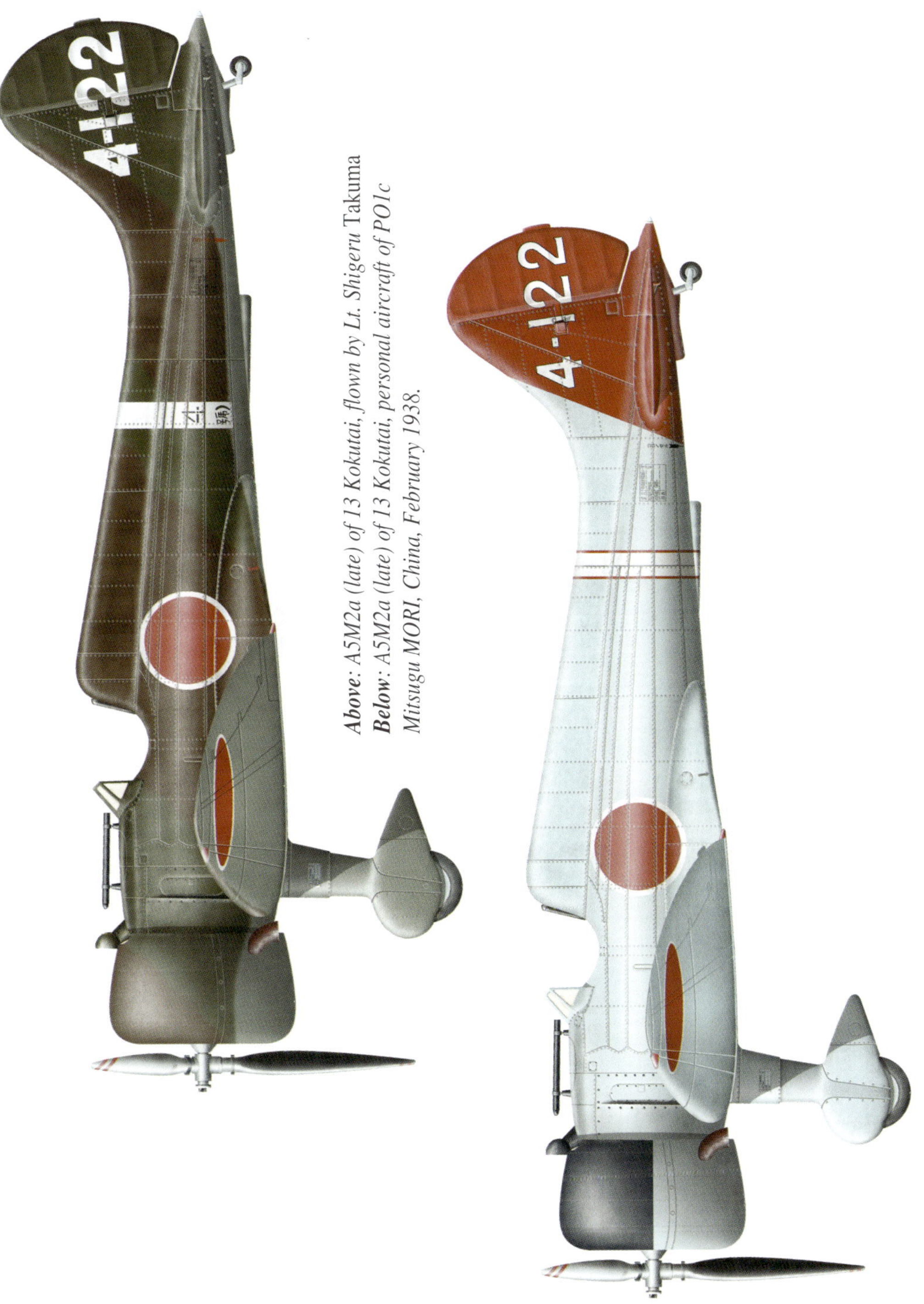

*Above*: A5M2a (late) of 13 Kokutai, flown by Lt. Shigeru Takuma
*Below*: A5M2a (late) of 13 Kokutai, personal aircraft of PO1c Mitsugu MORI, China, February 1938.

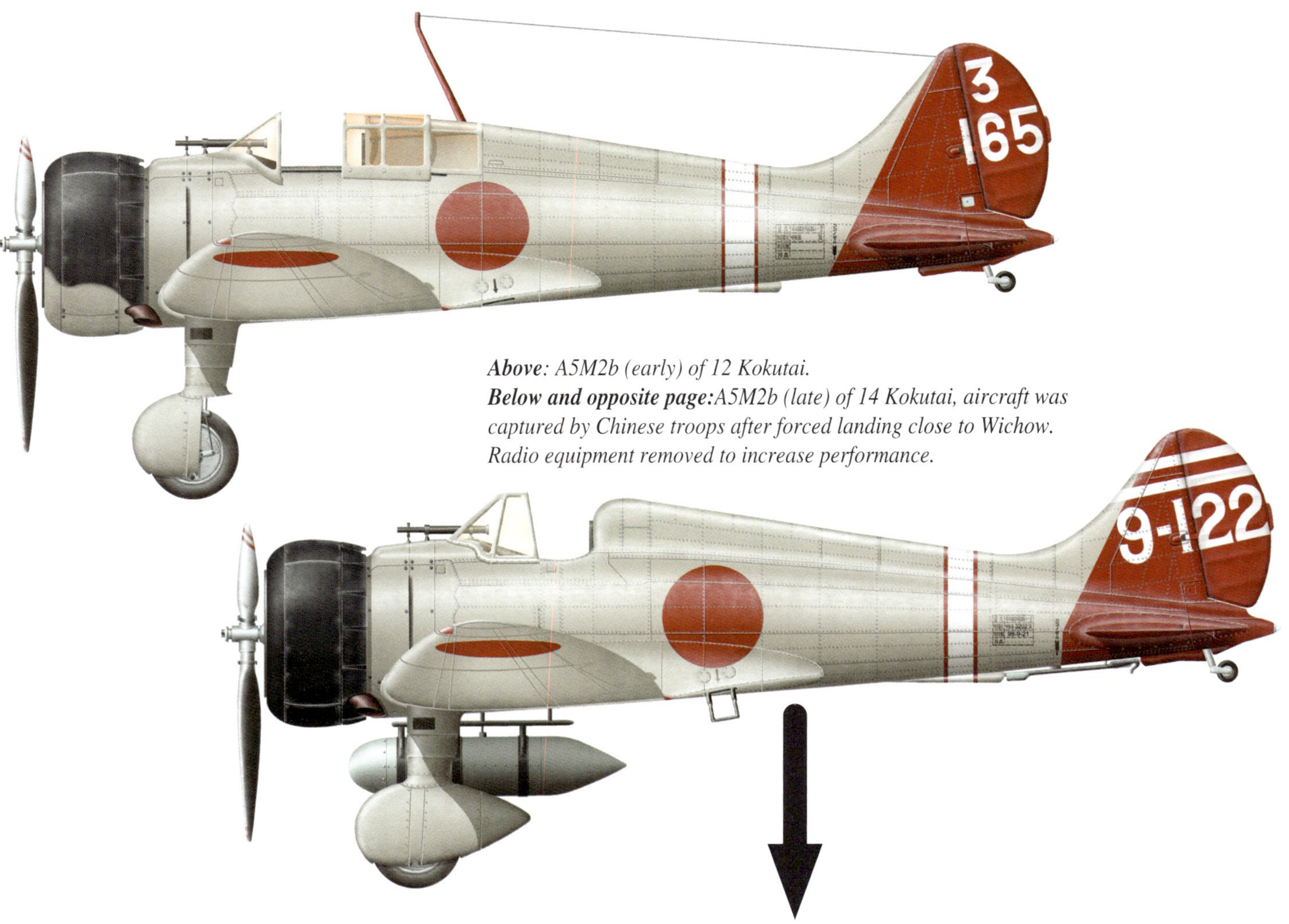

*Above*: A5M2b (early) of 12 Kokutai.
***Below and opposite page:***A5M2b (late) of 14 Kokutai, aircraft was captured by Chinese troops after forced landing close to Wichow. Radio equipment removed to increase performance.

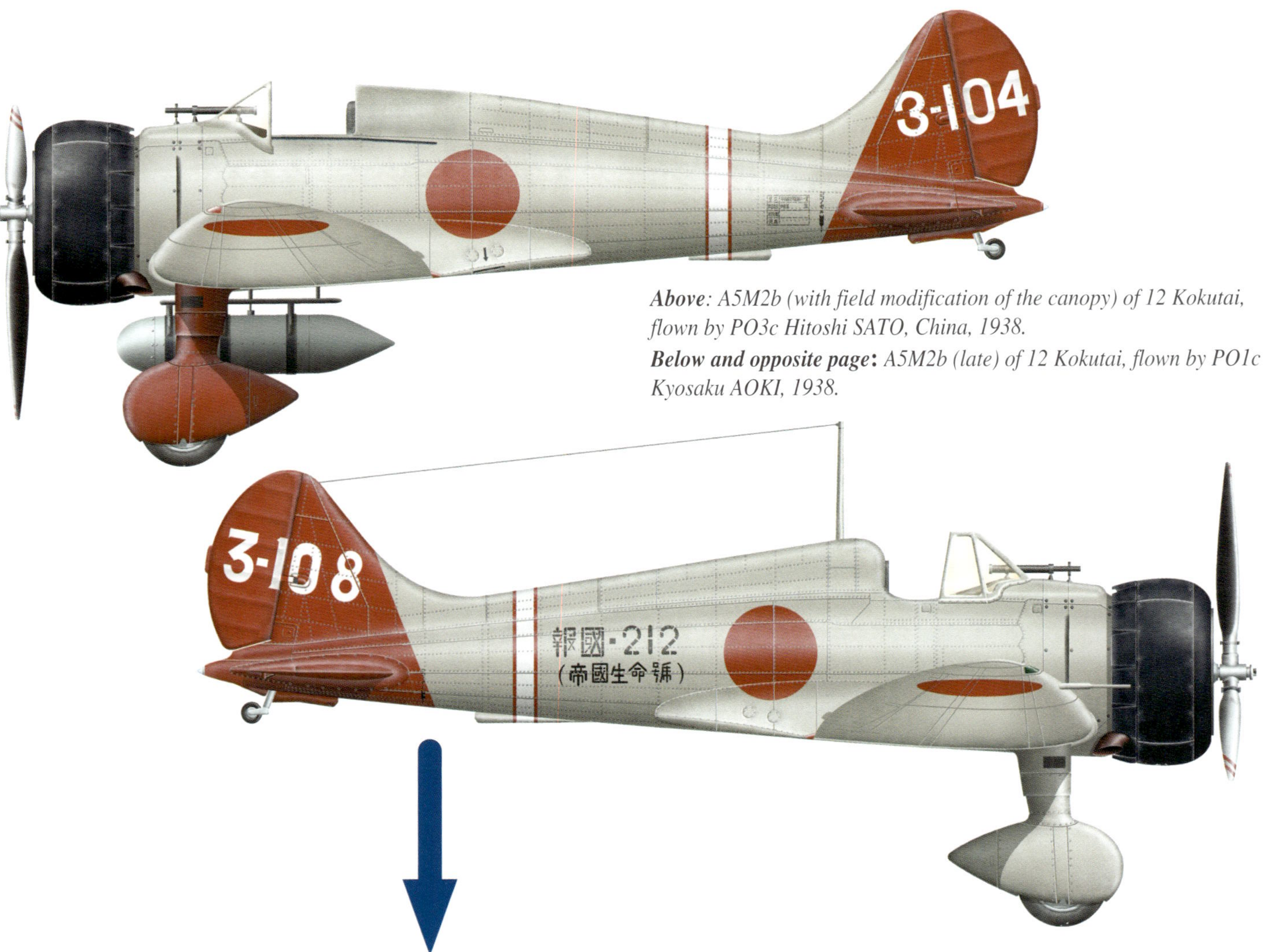

*Above*: A5M2b (with field modification of the canopy) of 12 Kokutai, flown by PO3c Hitoshi SATO, China, 1938.
**Below and opposite page:** A5M2b (late) of 12 Kokutai, flown by PO1c Kyosaku AOKI, 1938.

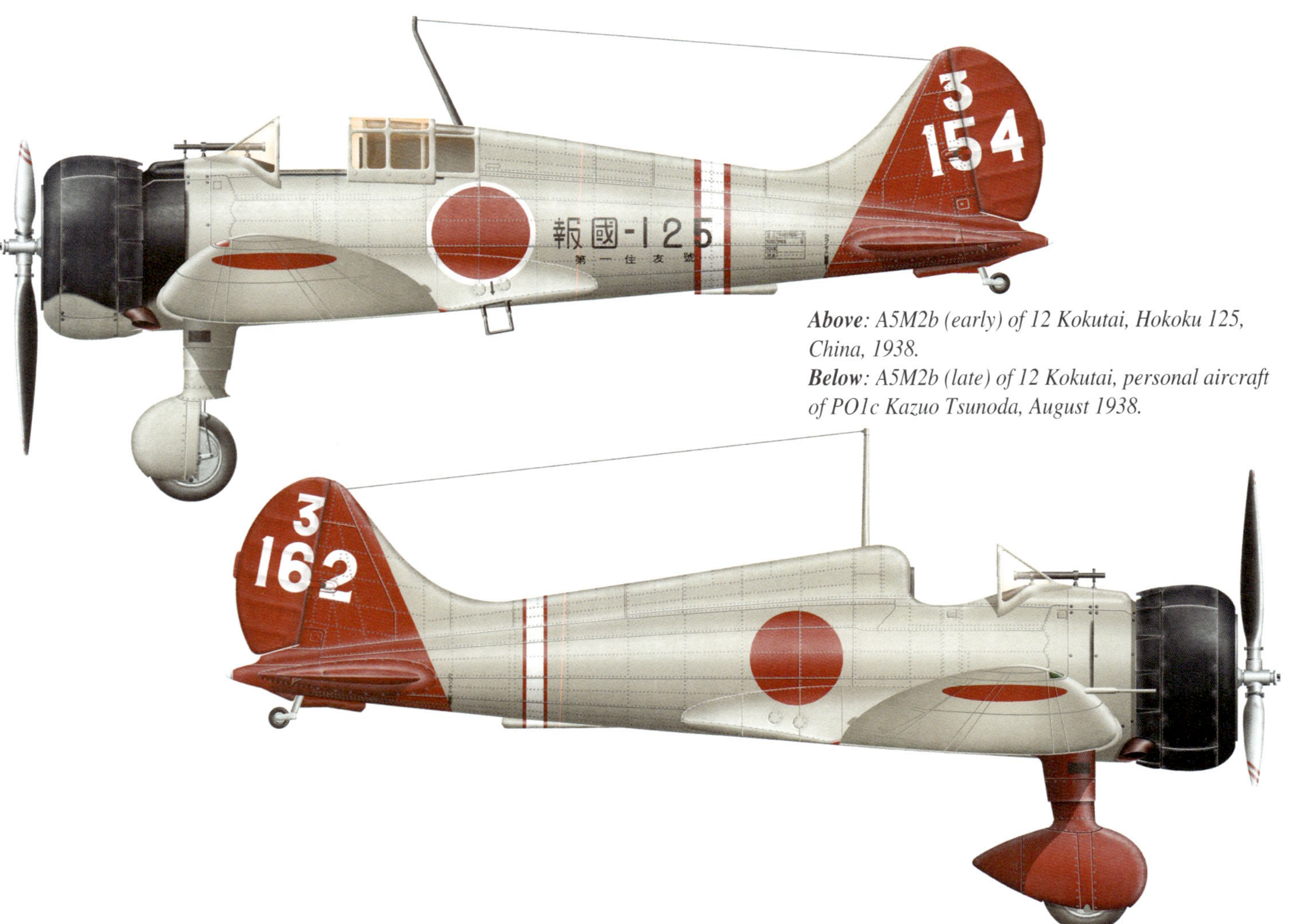

*Above*: A5M2b (early) of 12 Kokutai, Hokoku 125, China, 1938.
*Below*: A5M2b (late) of 12 Kokutai, personal aircraft of PO1c Kazuo Tsunoda, August 1938.

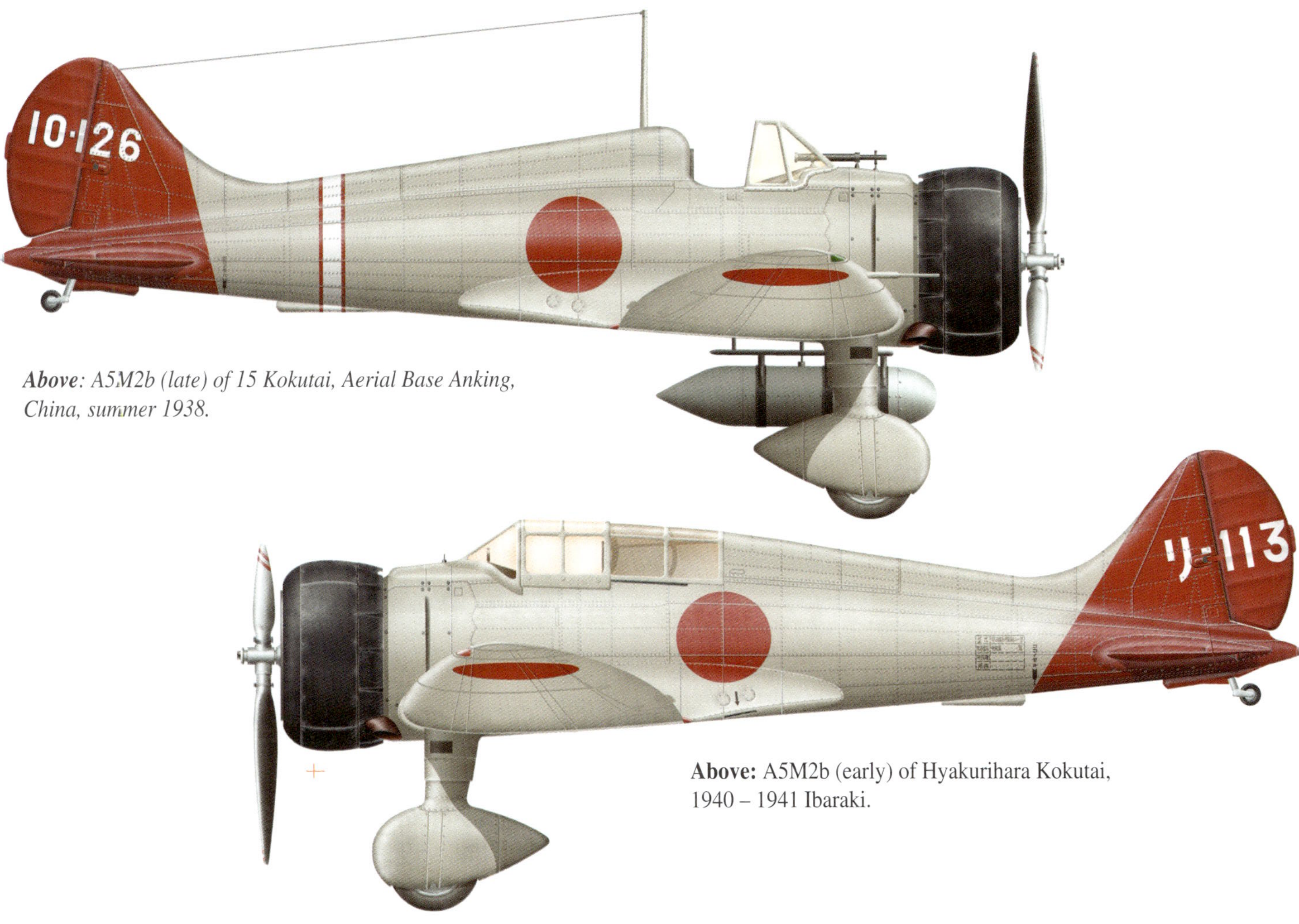

*Above*: A5M2b (late) of 15 Kokutai, Aerial Base Anking, China, summer 1938.

**Above:** A5M2b (early) of Hyakurihara Kokutai, 1940 – 1941 Ibaraki.

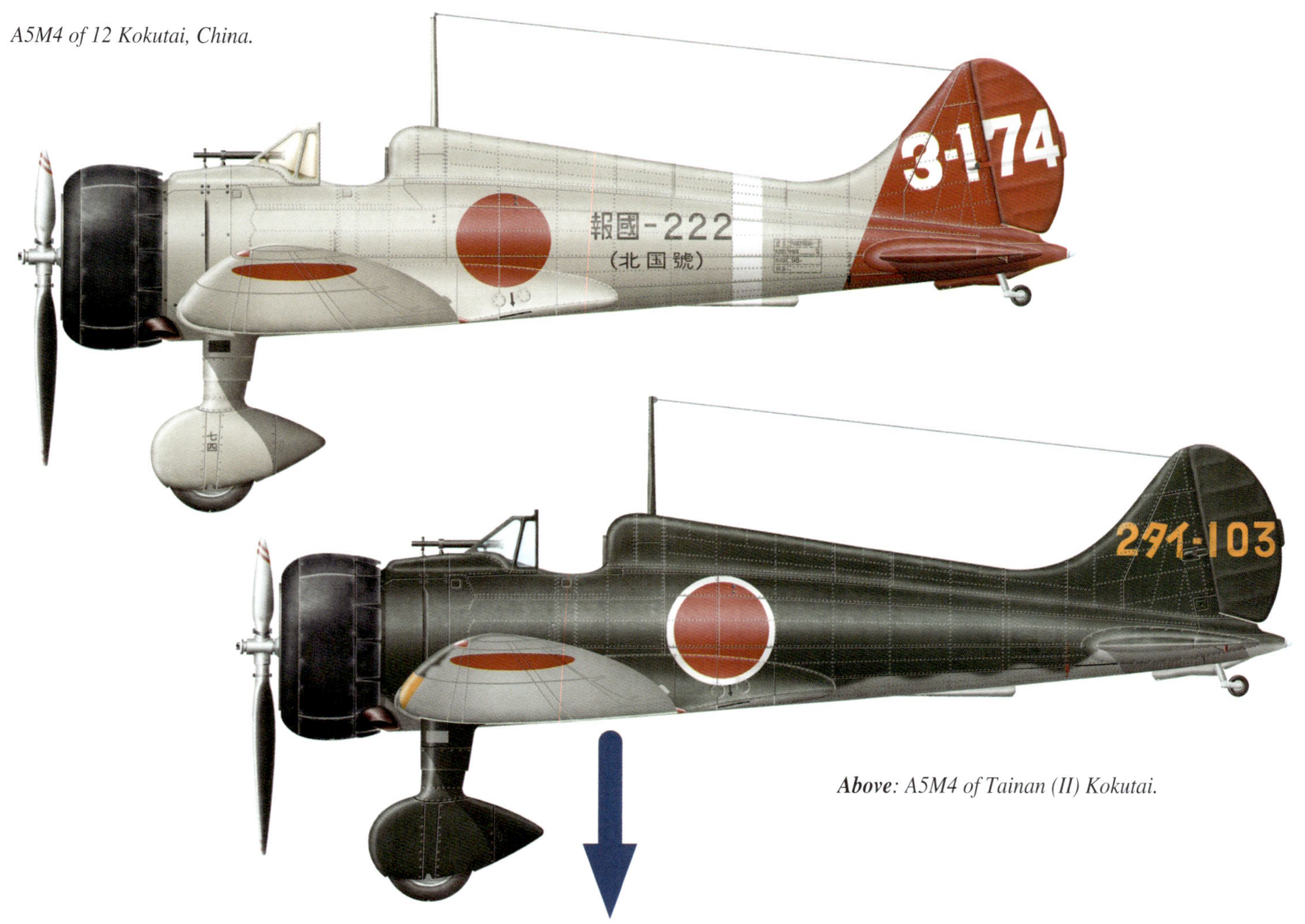

A5M4 of 12 Kokutai, China.

*Above*: A5M4 of Tainan (II) Kokutai.

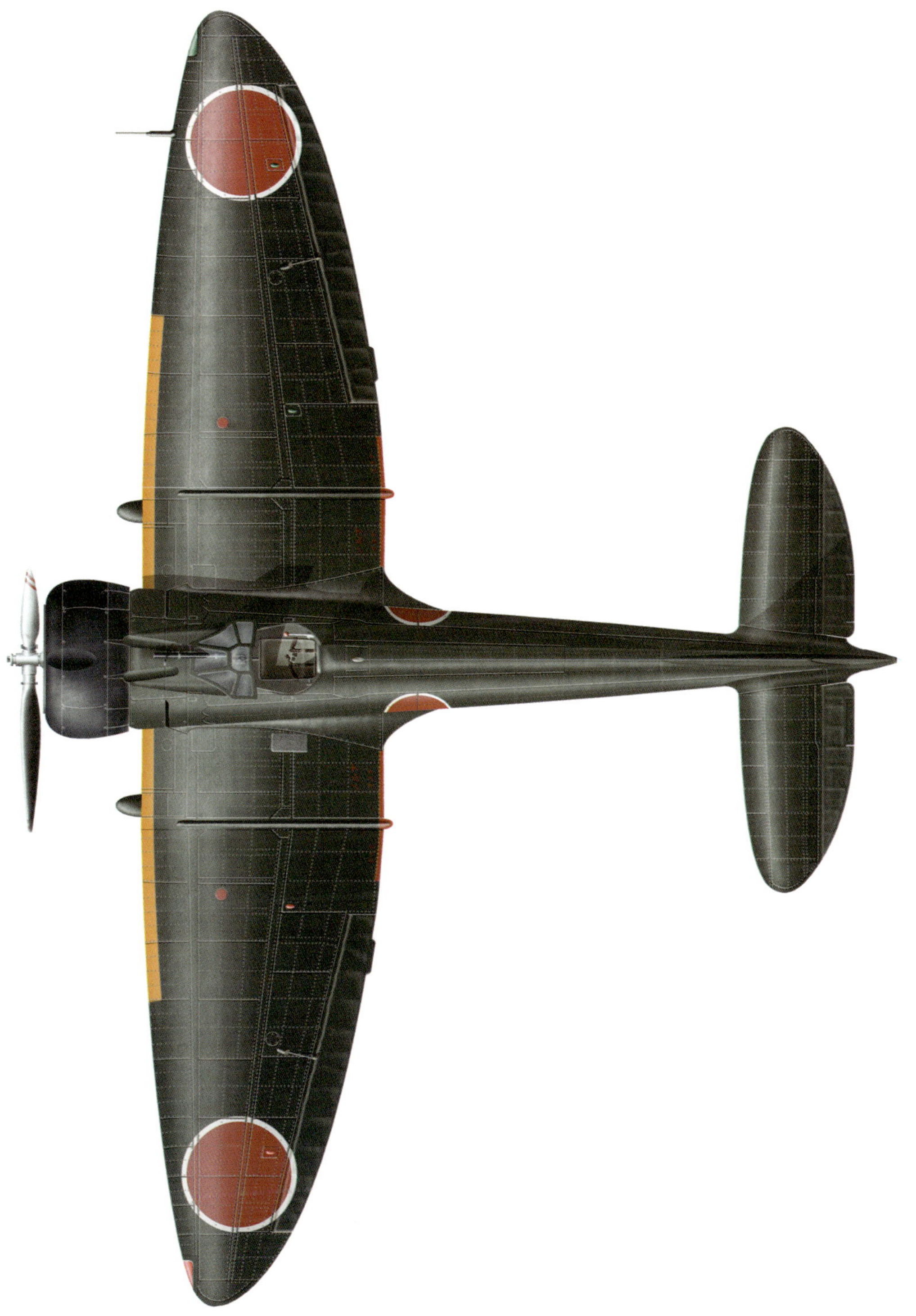

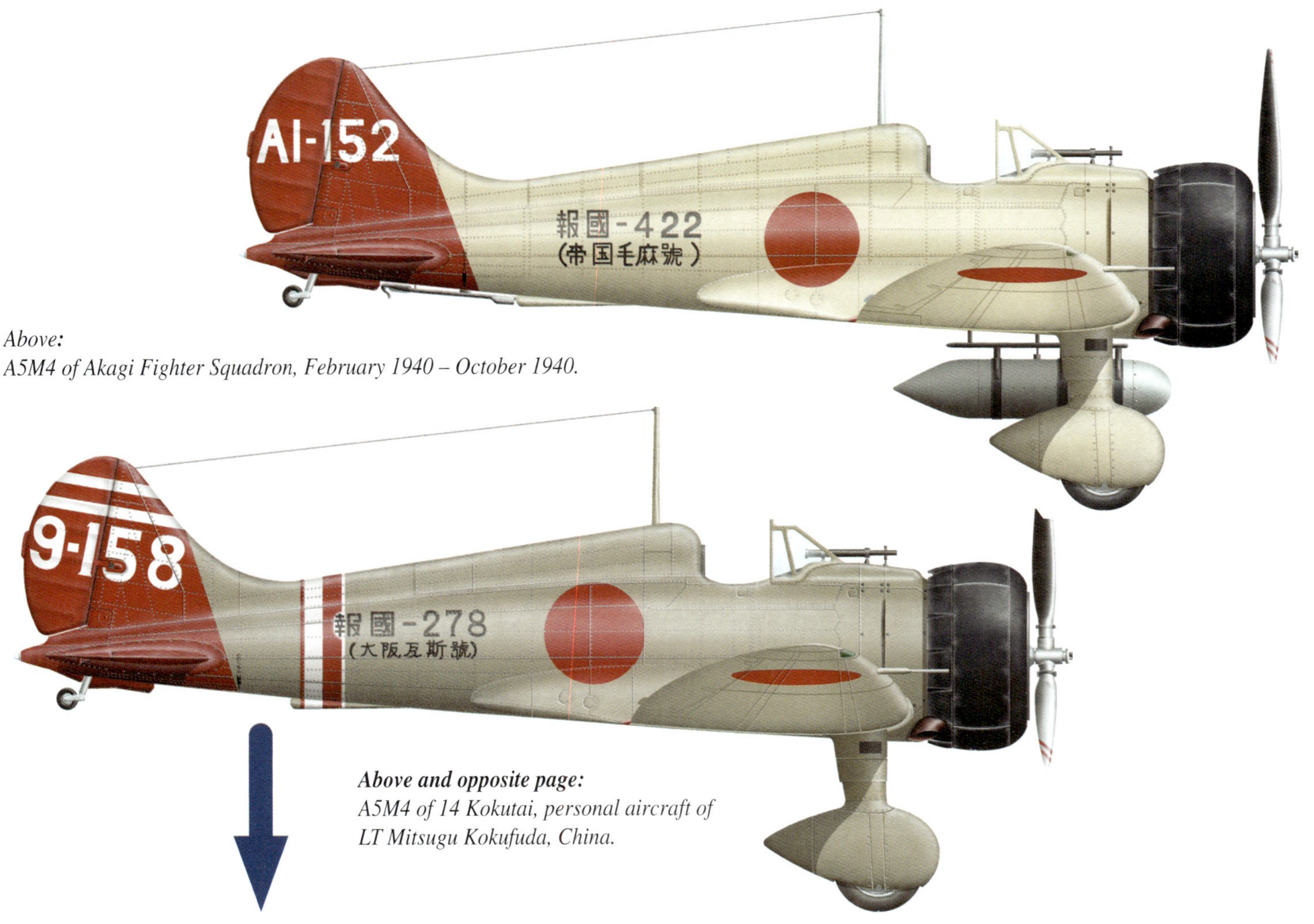

*Above:*
*A5M4 of Akagi Fighter Squadron, February 1940 – October 1940.*

***Above and opposite page:***
*A5M4 of 14 Kokutai, personal aircraft of*
*LT Mitsugu Kokufuda, China.*

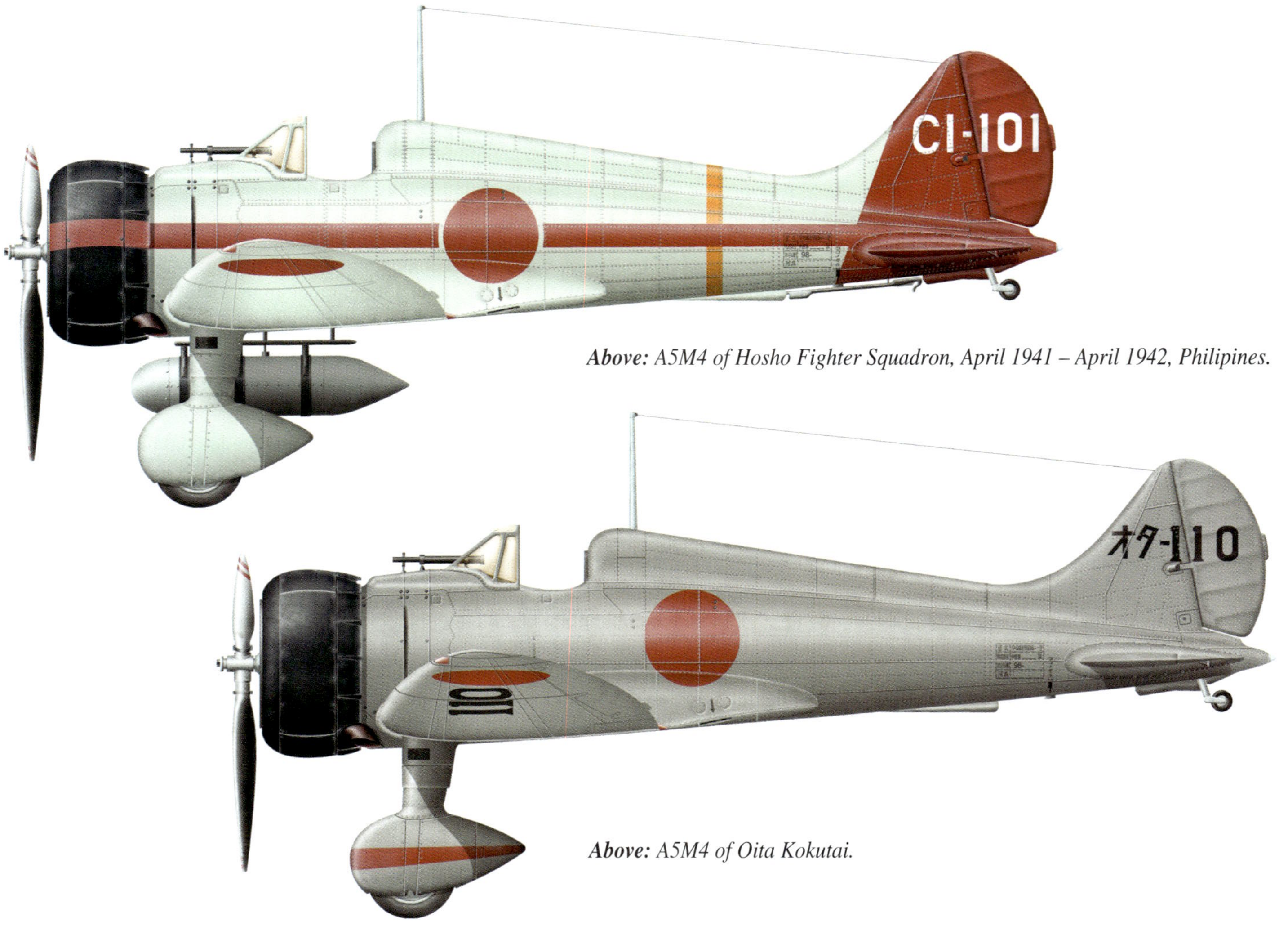

*Above: A5M4 of Hosho Fighter Squadron, April 1941 – April 1942, Philipines.*

*Above: A5M4 of Oita Kokutai.*

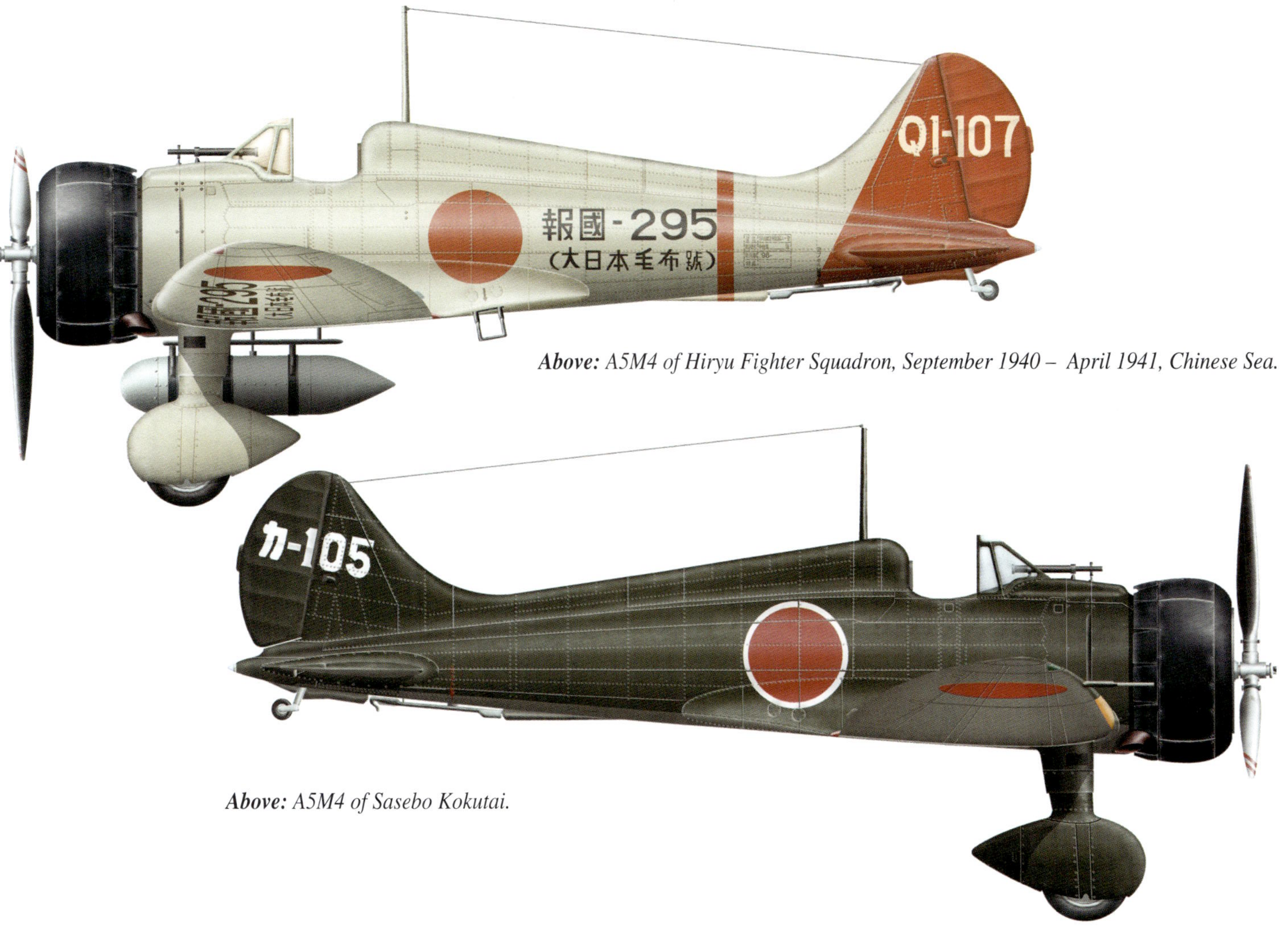

*Above:* A5M4 of Hiryu Fighter Squadron, September 1940 – April 1941, Chinese Sea.

*Above:* A5M4 of Sasebo Kokutai.

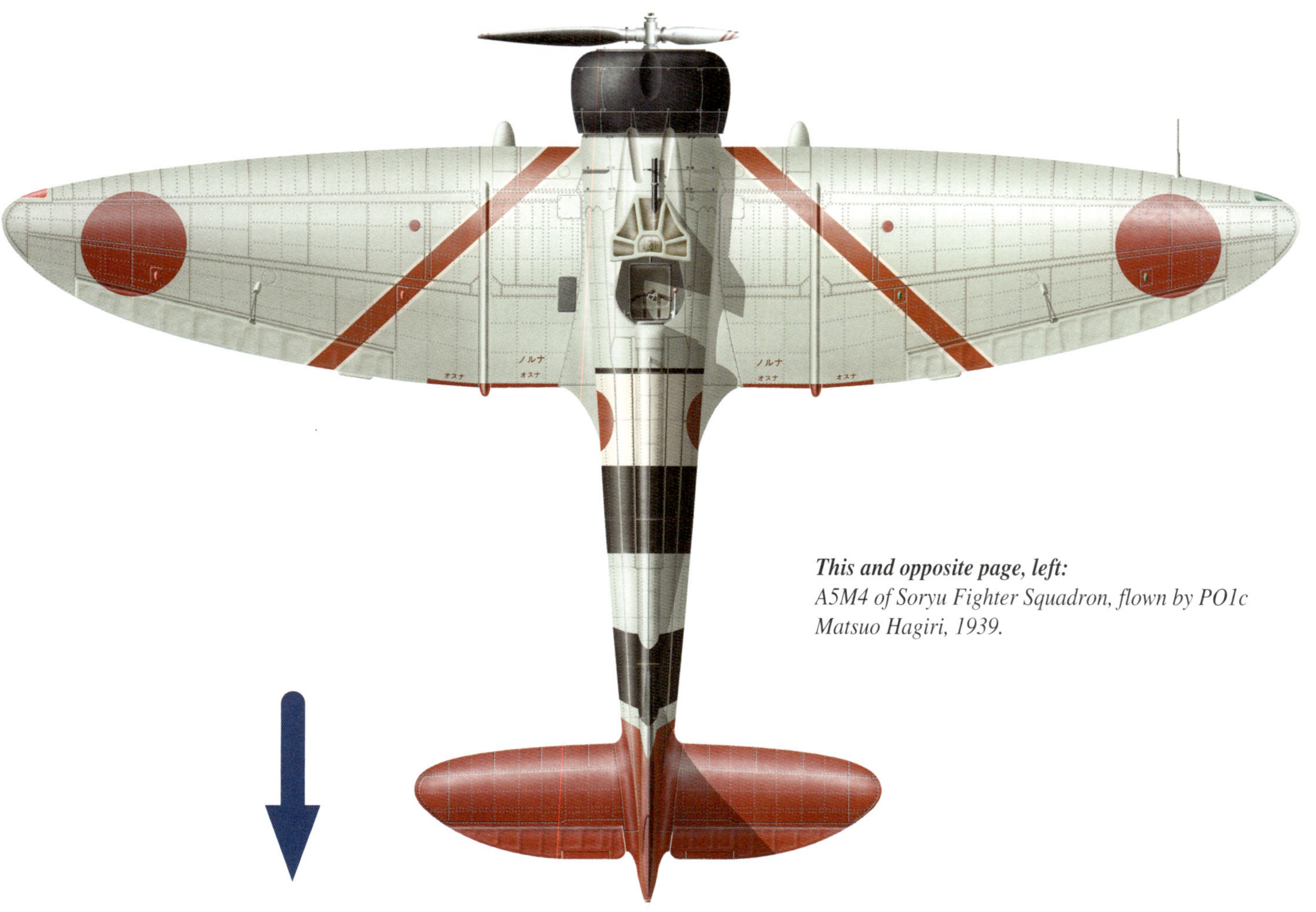

***This and opposite page, left:***
*A5M4 of Soryu Fighter Squadron, flown by PO1c*
*Matsuo Hagiri, 1939.*

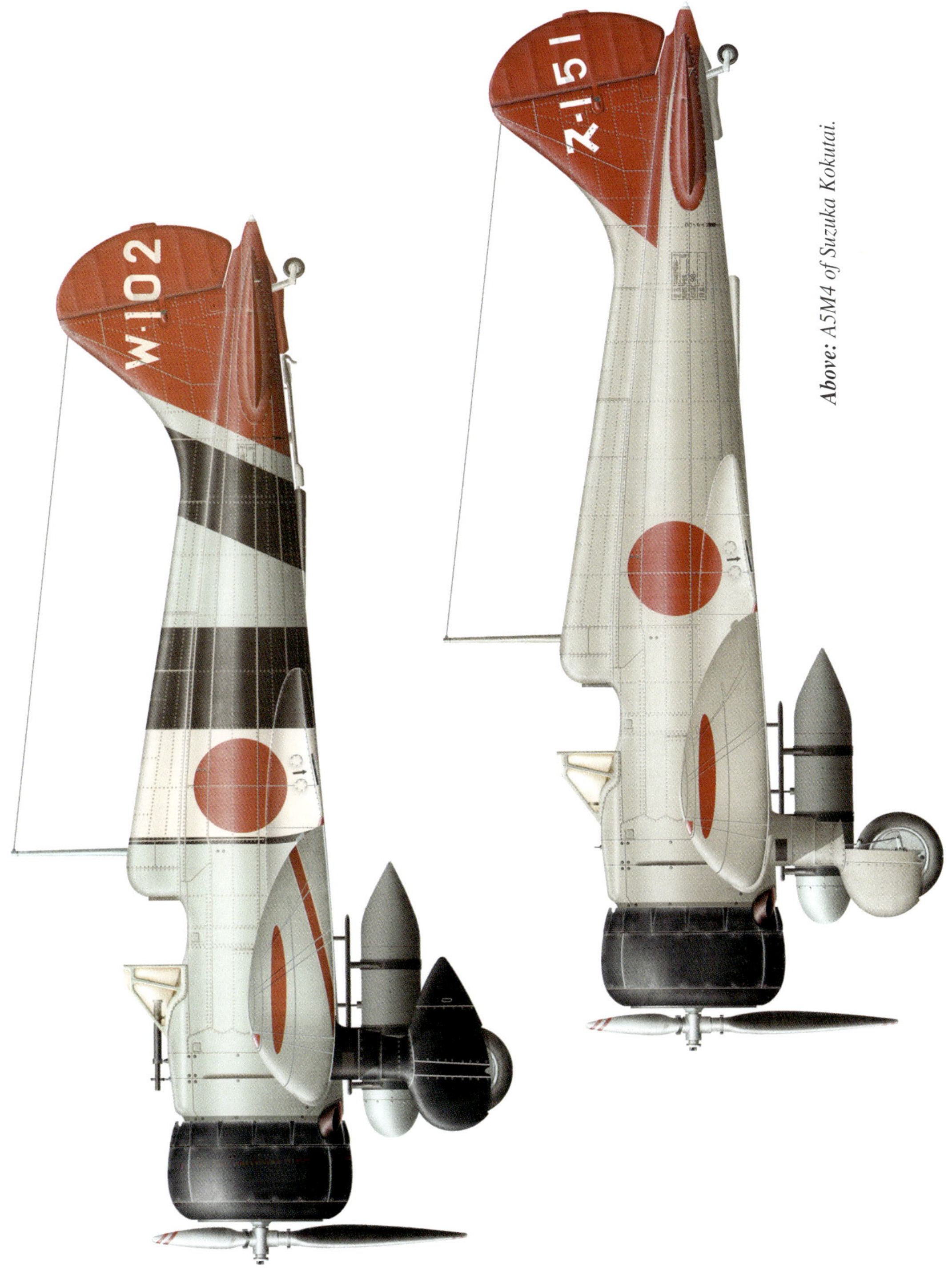

*Above: A5M4 of Suzuka Kokutai.*

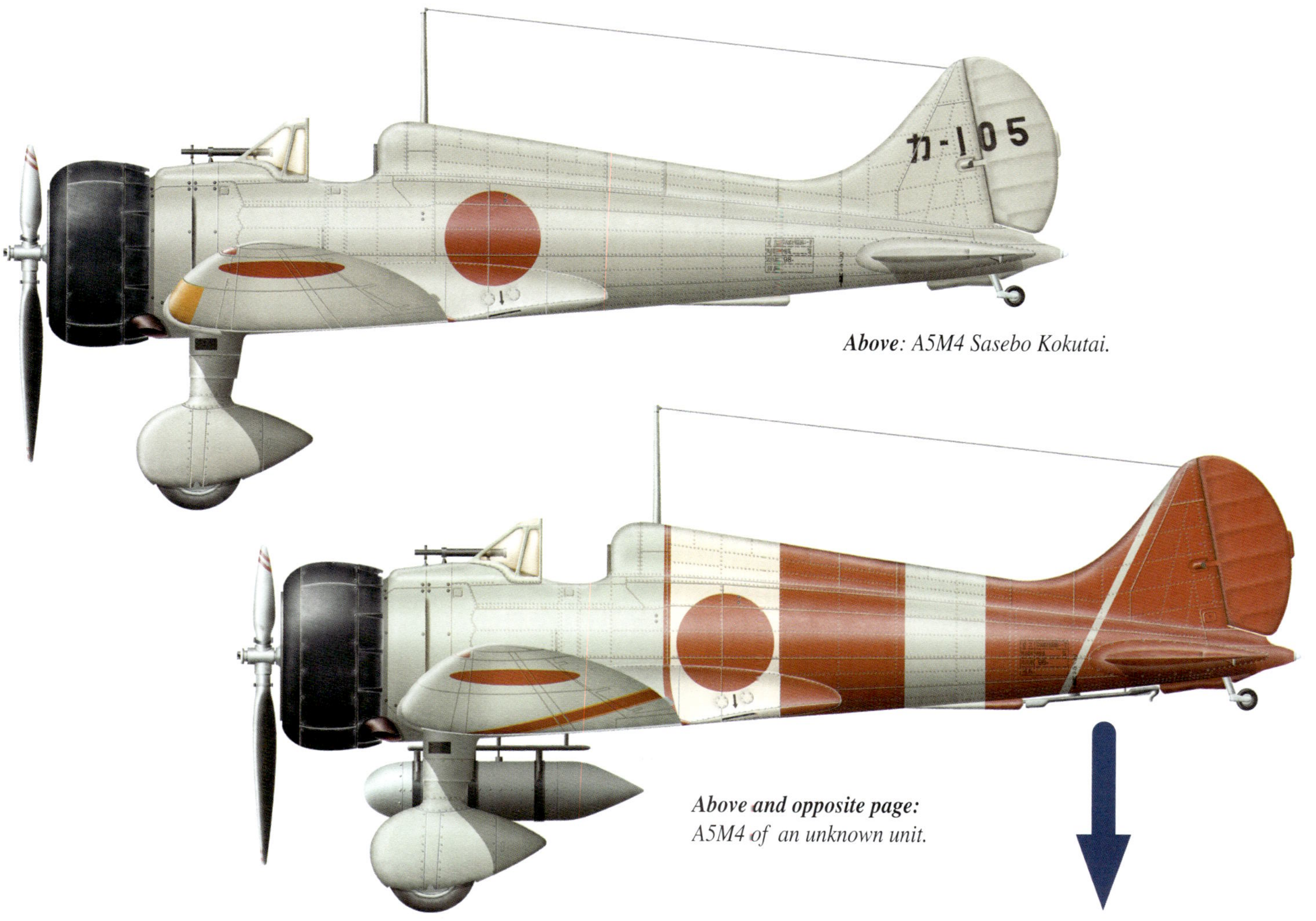

*Above*: A5M4 Sasebo Kokutai.

*Above and opposite page:*
A5M4 of an unknown unit.

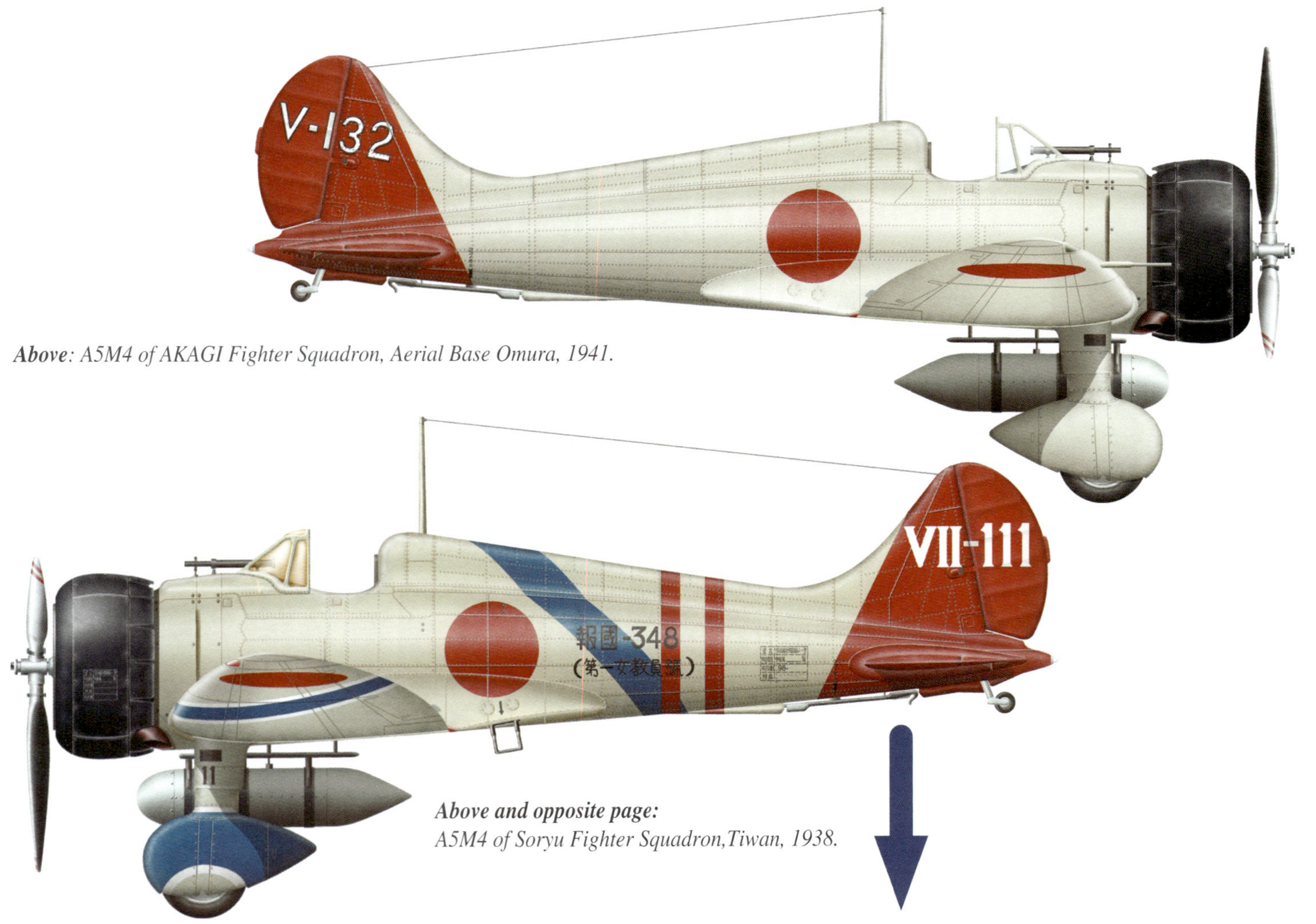

*Above: A5M4 of AKAGI Fighter Squadron, Aerial Base Omura, 1941.*

*Above and opposite page:*
*A5M4 of Soryu Fighter Squadron, Tiwan, 1938.*

*Mitsubishi A5M* **79**